TEA
SOMMELIER

*For Manuela, Nathanaëlle, Benoît, Paul, and Yann,
the very first students of the École du Thé. We celebrate
their commitment and enthusiasm, recognizing their
achievements and officially awarding them degrees
as accomplished tea sommeliers.*

*And for all the aspiring young tea sommeliers, to
encourage and support them on their journeys of
discovery.*

François-Xavier Delmas
Mathias Minet

TEA
SOMMELIER

✳ A STEP-BY-STEP GUIDE ✳

ABBEVILLE PRESS PUBLISHERS
NEW YORK LONDON

CONTENTS

INTRODUCING
THE TEA SOMMELIER

In recent years, tea has gained an enthusiastic audience around the world. This newfound popularity is evident in the level of consumption—which has tripled in the last twenty-five years—and in widespread interest in the subtleties of tea. Whether they are neophytes or connoisseurs, tea lovers are constantly seeking greater knowledge and more comprehensive guidance. Culinary professionals, including chefs, sommeliers, and restaurant owners, are demonstrating a desire to enhance their understanding of tea tasting, as well as the nuances of the culture of tea. We welcome all these aficionados, whose number is growing year by year, to the École du Thé.

Heightened expectations have driven a demand for quality, and the profession of tea sommelier has emerged as a result. The foremost mission of these newly minted specialists is to act as expert advisers. Their roles may include the design of customized tea menus and the pairing of teas with various foods. With the knowledgeable guidance of these professionals, tea is now a fixture on well-appointed tables, including those in the most sophisticated venues. Tea is making unexpected appearances, accompanying delicacies, perhaps sipped as an aperitif or complementing a tasting menu. Tea is also winning recognition in the best kitchens, featured as an ingredient in its own right. Whether you use it in infused, ground, crushed, or marinated form, opportunities to incorporate tea into recipes are limited only by the cook's imagination.

Renowned experts devote themselves to the subtleties of wine connoisseurship, and a vast literature has made the topic accessible to a broad audience. Surely tea deserves the same level of recognition.

In this book, we provide a straightforward approach to learning that will lead you step by step, allowing you to master the complexities of tea. Each page is designed to serve as a brief lesson on a specific topic. Whether you have a couple of minutes or an hour, you'll learn something new about tea every time you open this book. Feel free to pick and choose, gleaning bits of information as you flip from page to page, following your inclinations and interests.

Our goal is to help you explore the world of tea with confidence and ease. We hope this book will also lead you to further discoveries, deepening your knowledge and—perhaps—inspiring some of our readers to pursue careers as tea sommeliers.

Meanwhile, why not experiment at home in the simplest way possible? Enjoy yourself while discovering the inner secrets of the trade and put them into practice for the pleasure of your friends and family.

SELECTING
AND
PREPARING
TEA

TEA FOR EVERY TIME OF DAY

*Teas vary widely in their flavors, qualities, and effects on the mind and body.
Some teas are particularly appropriate at certain times of day.
Some varieties demand special time and attention and are not well suited to early morning
consumption. Others have a distinctive aromatic finesse whose subtlety is best appreciated
when sampled as an aperitif rather than being served at the end of a meal.
Varieties that are lower in caffeine are perfect for evening refreshment.*

FOR A GENTLE START TO THE DAY

A shaded tea, such as Gyokuro Hikari, served at body temperature for healthy hydration as the day begins

FOR A ROUSING WAKE-UP CALL

A strong black tea, such as Yunnan d'Or, to organize your thoughts, hydrate your system, and stimulate your mind and body

AT THE END OF A LONG DAY

A low-caffeine oolong, such as Da Hong Pao, to help you relax for a good night's sleep

FOR AN APERITIF

An oolong that's both buttery and herbal, Anxi Tie Guan Yin, to stimulate the appetite and tantalize the taste buds

FOR BRUNCH

A strong smoky tea, such as Lapsang Souchong or Thé du Tigre, the perfect accompaniment for both sweets and savories

AT TEATIME

A Yunnan black tea or a Blue of London Earl Grey, delicately flavored with bergamot, for the ritual of five o'clock tea

FOR HEALTHY DIGESTION

Pu Erh Imperial, a dark tea, beneficial for digestion, helping you to slenderize and lowering cholesterol

AT WORK

A light and lively brew, a first flush Darjeeling, to stimulate your mental synapses

TEA FOR EVERY SEASON

Each sip of tea is an evocation of nature and the rhythmic passage of the seasons.
In every cup, you'll find fragrant echoes of herbs, flowers, fruits, or the moist turf of a woodland glade.
It's delightful to match these aromatic notes to the seasons of the year.

SPRING

Consider a newly harvested variety, perhaps a first flush Darjeeling or Nepal, a fresh green China tea, or a Japanese Ichibancha. All offer distinctive vegetal notes (sprouts, fresh-cut grass, spinach) that echo nature's reawakening.

SUMMER

Try a light green tea, such as a summer Darjeeling or Nepal, cold brewed to provide cool refreshment and intriguingly varied flavors.

AUTUMN

We suggest a green tea, such as Jasmine Pearls, if you'd like to extend the summer break and defer the advent of autumn. Otherwise, a tea with a woodsy aroma, such as a Taiwan Oolong or a Qimen Mao Feng, redolent of leather and cocoa, will immerse you in the season and prompt you to consider a forest outing.

WINTER

Try a black tea with warm notes, a dark tea, or a variety with the flavors of spices, cocoa, or mellow fruit compotes: a Pu Erh, a Yunnan Buds Premium, a Korean Jukro, or an African grand cru will offer warmth and comfort.

TEA THAT TAKES YOU ON A JOURNEY

Tea invites you to venture on an exotic voyage, transporting you to distant lands and lofty heights. Close your eyes as you take the first sip and allow yourself to be spirited away to faraway destinations. Imagine yourself in another world, as a geisha, a monk, an explorer, or a patrician lady.

TANGIER
A welcoming glass of green tea scented with mint

KYOTO
Fleur de Geisha, a green tea scented with cherry blossoms

BEIJING
Thé des Concubines, a tea to enjoy in languorous repose

MUMBAI
Imperial Chai, a spiced tea

ISTANBUL
Thé du Hammam, a tea to relish while pampering your body

COLOMBO
A New Vithanakande tea from a boutique producer

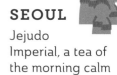

SEOUL
Jejudo Imperial, a tea of the morning calm

LHASA
Thé des Moines, a tea that transports you from worldly cares

NAIROBI
Thé des Amants, a black tea flavored with ginger

LONDON
Thé des Lords, a tea that's correct for all occasions

TEA FOR
WINE AFICIONADOS

There are many similarities between the worlds of tea and wine. Both cultures embrace the concepts of varietals, climates, soils, pedigrees, and vintages, and both demand a certain savoir faire. Technical vocabularies and tasting practices also have points in common. Finally, tannins play an important role in many teas and wines.

CHAMPAGNE

An AV2 first flush Darjeeling for its exquisite finesse

ARMAGNAC

A vintage Pu Erh for its ability to develop complexity and mellowness from aging

WHITE WINES WITH MINERAL FLAVORS

A Lu An Gua Pian for its flinty notes

HEAVY WHITE WINES

A Jin Xuan or an Anxi Tie Guan Yin for their buttery, floral, luscious notes

FULL RED WINES WITH WOODSY, SPICY NOTES

A Yunnan Buds Premium with hints of resinous wood, oak moss, and honey

DRY WHITE WINES

A Nepalese green tea for cool refreshment

TANNIC RED WINES

An Assam Maijian for its distinctive structure

SWEET WHITE WINES

A traditional tea from Taiwan that offers a rich texture and honeyed notes

KIR

A flavored tea that will evoke a delightful blend of fragrances

LIGHT RED WINES

A New Vithanakande from Sri Lanka for its light texture and pleasing apple and honey notes

TEA FOR EVERY PERSONALITY TYPE

It's fun to select a tea that's just right for the friend you're planning to share it with. Tell me who you are, and I'll select the correct tea. The range is vast, but you can enjoy playing variations on a game of twenty questions to help you decide.

FOR YOUR SWEETHEART

A spiced tea—why not a Thé des Amants?

FOR A FREE SPIRIT

A tea that's redolent of the Larzac region, with notes of the stable, damp wood, and moist straw: a Pu Erh

FOR THE CLUB-GOING SET

An invigorating brew full of buds—perhaps a first flush Darjeeling or a tea that "sweats" a little during the processing stage, such as a Taiwan Oolong or a Dong Ding

FOR A SMOKER

A smoky brew, perhaps a Thé du Tigre

FOR A YOGA TEACHER

A tea that inspires well-being and serenity. Perhaps a Japanese green tea, such as Ryokucha Midori.

FOR YOUR BIKER FRIEND

A tea with leather notes, a Qimen or a Jukro

FOR A RESPECTABLE LADY—YOUR GRANDMOTHER, PERHAPS

A great, politically correct classic, perhaps a Blue of London Earl Grey

FOR A COFFEE DRINKER

A tea with a roasted aroma to make her forget about espresso. Try a Hojicha—a Shiraore Kuki Hojicha

FOR A MARTIAL ARTS FAN

A tea prepared by the Gong Fu Cha method, with absolute mastery—a Feng Huang Dan Cong Oolong

FOR A TEENAGER

A cheeky brew, infused in a blend of milk and water—a Masala Chai

FOR YOUR ROOMIE

A convivial and welcoming selection that's like a bouquet of flowers—a cold-brewed jasmine tea, easy to prepare and whimsically presented in a stemmed glass

TEA FOR EVERY OCCASION

When you present tea as a gift, you demonstrate your own taste and imagination as well as honoring the recipient. Select a pretty caddy wrapped in Japanese paper, a container crafted from cherry bark, or a simply painted canister.
Tea is considered a symbol of hospitality and is an esteemed gift in many countries.

FOR A WEDDING

A lovely teapot to be treasured for a lifetime, with a pair of cups and a grand cru tea selection

FOR VISITING FRIENDS

A tea that tastes yummy with macarons

FOR DINNER IN TOWN

An unfamiliar tea variety with posh associations that will tantalize the imagination

FOR A BIRTHDAY

As many types of tea as candles on the cake

FOR A STAY WITH FRIENDS

A handsome package with a different tea for each day of your visit

FOR A FAREWELL GIFT FOR A DEPARTING COLLEAGUE

A nice assortment of various teas

FOR MOTHER'S DAY

A tea chosen with loving care

IN BULK OR IN BAGS?

*Tea bags were introduced in the United States in the early twentieth century.
They revolutionized tea consumption in the West, and they've since taken over the world.
As a result, many of us have forgotten that a good tea is made from whole leaves; their delicate
structure should never be subjected to the destructive crushing that's required to fill tea bags.*

TEA BAGS VERSUS QUALITY

When tea bags were first developed and marketed, the idea was simply to package a few whole tea leaves in paper packets. But this practice proved to be slow and complicated; it wasn't long before the tea was being processed in grinders and reduced to a fine dust. This efficient technique certainly facilitated the production of teabags, but at the cost of a precipitous decline in quality.

Tea that is broken or pulverized becomes much stronger as it brews in the cup; finely chopped leaves release a lot of "heavy" tannins **to the detriment of a tea's aromatic delicacy.**

too flat, too bitter, too astringent, lacking aroma

FINE MESH

⋈

In the 1980s, merchants began to package tea in little bags of natural cotton mesh that can accommodate whole tea leaves. They are a relatively high-quality option for use in planes, hotels, and, more generally, in situations where it may be difficult to find good tea.

THE TYRANNY OF COLOR

Over time, marketers have altered tea bag contents in response to the sacrosanct yet ill-conceived notion of "consumer expectations." These consumers, it was said, expected color in their cups; you could see it in the way they frantically jiggled the tea bag, as if depth of color correlated with good flavor. The tea industry therefore began to fill their tea bags with ever more finely chopped leaves that release their deeply colored tannins almost instantaneously.

Needless to say, these tea bags have no place whatsoever in the teapots or cups of any tea lover, nor should they appear on any tea menu worthy of the name.

CONTACT WITH WATER

The preparation of tea consists of placing the leaves in contact with water. The soluble components in the tea leaves are dissolved by the action of water and heat and migrate into the liquor, converting to a so-called aqueous phase. To brew a fine cup of tea, this contact between the leaves and the water must occur under optimal conditions.

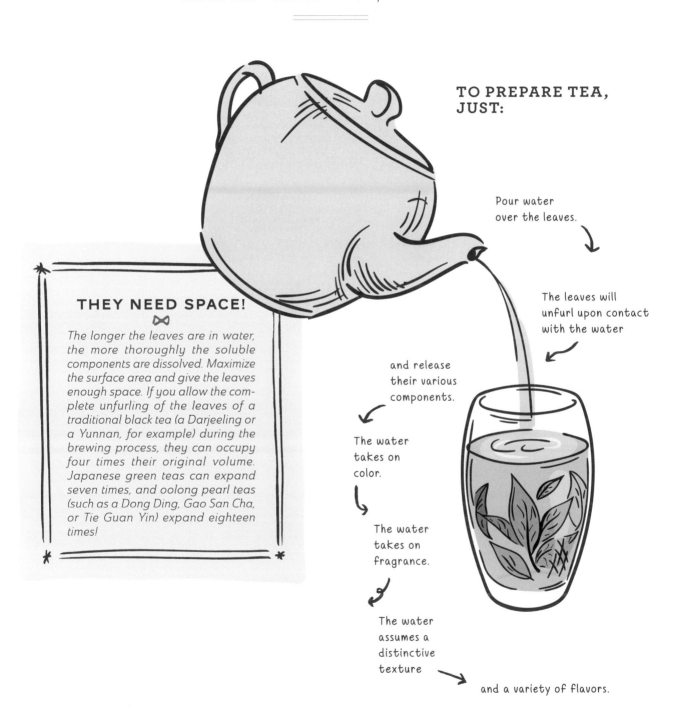

TO PREPARE TEA, JUST:

Pour water over the leaves.

The leaves will unfurl upon contact with the water

and release their various components.

The water takes on color.

The water takes on fragrance.

The water assumes a distinctive texture

and a variety of flavors.

THEY NEED SPACE!

The longer the leaves are in water, the more thoroughly the soluble components are dissolved. Maximize the surface area and give the leaves enough space. If you allow the complete unfurling of the leaves of a traditional black tea (a Darjeeling or a Yunnan, for example) during the brewing process, they can occupy four times their original volume. Japanese green teas can expand seven times, and oolong pearl teas (such as a Dong Ding, Gao San Cha, or Tie Guan Yin) expand eighteen times!

MEASURING TEA

You should determine the amount of tea leaves you'll need based on the capacity of your teapot. The more leaves you use, the more intense the flavors will be (see pages 20 and 55), and the liquor's taste may become unbalanced. There is no specific rule for measuring tea, but there are two major schools of thought on the subject.

THE WESTERN APPROACH...

In Western measurement, the typical ratio of leaves to water is between 1:5 and 1:7. **This is the traditional recommended guideline of 1 teaspoon/2 g of leaves per cup or 3.5 to 5 ounces/100 to 150 ml of water.** If this volume is increased, the proportion will decrease to 1:10.

...OR THE CHINESE METHOD?

Measurements in China reflect the utensils used there (miniature Gong Fu Cha and Zhong teapots) and approach the question more in terms of volume than weight. **The leaves should take up 20 to 50 percent of the capacity of the teapot or cup.**

CURRENT TRENDS

We have noticed that tea lovers are tending to increase the amount of tea and shorten the infusion time. This approach has the effect of raising the concentration of aromatic components (which are readily water soluble), particularly those that are responsible for a tea's volatile top notes, creating a strong initial olfactory impression. But there is a risk: increasing the concentration of tannins can produce astringency and bitterness, disrupting the liquor's balance.

Western
measurement:
1:5 to 1:10

Chinese
measurement:
3:10 to 5:10

REMINDER
⋈

* *Measure the capacity of your teapot.*

* *A teacup holds about 3.5 ounces/100 ml.*

* *Use the equivalent of 1 teaspoon/2 g of leaves per cup.*

* *Tea prepared without enough leaves tastes like dishwater.*

* *An overly strong brew will have an unpleasant mouthfeel, with unbalanced aromas and textures.*

CHOOSING THE RIGHT WATER

Water plays an essential role in the quality of tea. To understand its effect, try preparing your usual tea with water from a different source. You'll immediately taste the difference. You may have already noticed that your favorite tea has a different flavor depending on whether you're drinking it in the city or the country.

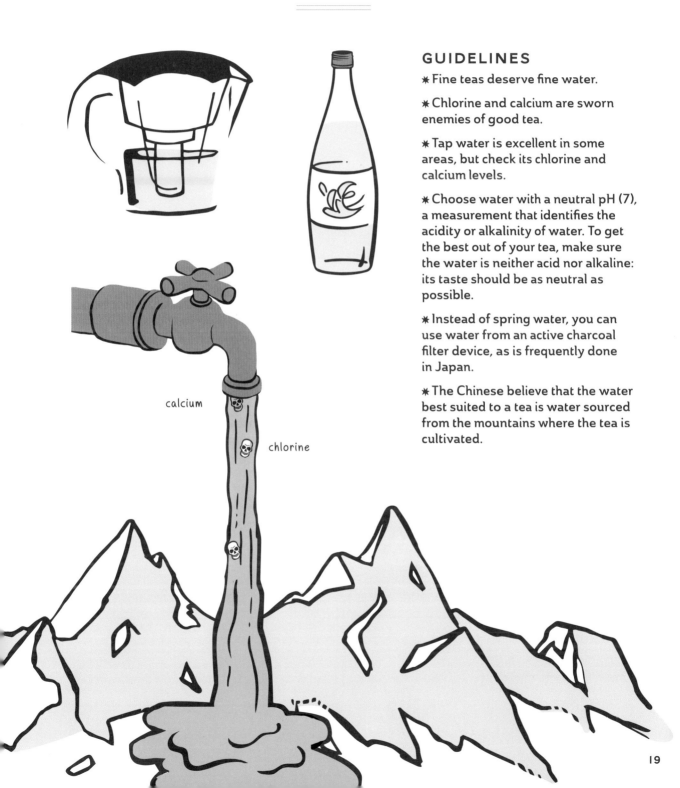

calcium

chlorine

GUIDELINES

✳ Fine teas deserve fine water.

✳ Chlorine and calcium are sworn enemies of good tea.

✳ Tap water is excellent in some areas, but check its chlorine and calcium levels.

✳ Choose water with a neutral pH (7), a measurement that identifies the acidity or alkalinity of water. To get the best out of your tea, make sure the water is neither acid nor alkaline: its taste should be as neutral as possible.

✳ Instead of spring water, you can use water from an active charcoal filter device, as is frequently done in Japan.

✳ The Chinese believe that the water best suited to a tea is water sourced from the mountains where the tea is cultivated.

BREWING AT THE RIGHT TEMPERATURE

Each tea infuses differently in water. Some green teas should never be exposed to water heated to over 122°F/50°C, but a black tea, such as a high-grown Sri Lanka, will only yield its best when brewed with water over 194°F/90°C. There's an ideal brewing temperature for each type of tea.

A QUESTION OF BALANCE

Heat facilitates the release of most of the components found in tea leaves—the hotter the water, the more they migrate into the solution—but heat also destroys or alters some of these elements.

This important point cannot be overemphasized. **A well-brewed tea does not necessarily contain the maximum amount of these components; instead, it offers a balance of tannins, amino acids, and aromatic elements.**

Monitoring the water temperature allows you to control this balance. Since every tea is distinct, the proper temperature will vary. There's an optimal temperature for every type of tea.

EVERY HOME NEEDS ONE!

An electric teakettle with a thermostat is an indispensable appliance for every tea lover. It enables you to brew your tea at exactly the recommended temperature and avoid the nuisance of boiling water on the stove.

BOILED WATER IS BAD WATER

Water should never actually boil, and this maxim applies to every type of tea. As water heats, the gases in the air dissolved in the water, including oxygen, gradually evaporate. At 104°F/40°C, you'll see fine bubbles begin to form. These gases are released throughout the heating process, and when the water comes to a full boil, all of the oxygen evaporates. But this gas plays an important role in flavor; it facilitates the transmission of aromatic components into a gaseous state and thus the sensation experienced in the olfactory bulb (see page 41).

LENGTH OF THE INFUSION TIME

No doubt you've experienced a disagreeable taste that made you grimace at the first sip of overbrewed tea. But do you understand its source?

GUIDELINES

Tea leaves release their various components (caffeine, tannins, etc.) into the water at different rates.

Caffeine is released very quickly: 80 percent in the first minute of infusion.

Tannins are released more slowly: it takes 7 minutes for 80 percent of them to dissolve.

Aromas have their own release rate depending on their molecular composition.

THE CLOCK IS TICKING...

If you let the tea leaves steep too long, these components may dissolve to excess. The tea may become bitter or astringent, for example. You must halt the infusion process at the moment when the liquor is at its most finely balanced—when the aromas, textures, and flavors are in harmony.

In other words, there's an ideal infusion time for each and every tea, depending on the tea variety and preparation method (see pages 20 and 22).

THE COLOR OF THE LIQUOR

The color of the tea in your cup is no indicator of the appropriate duration of the infusion. Each tea variety has its own distinct color and intensity. Some teas with very low levels of pigments, including green and white varieties, produce very clear pale liquors.

RECOMMENDED BREWING TIMES

The proper infusion time for teas ranges from 10 seconds to 8 minutes.
It's essential to know the proper brewing times and temperatures
for your favorite teas.

WHITE TEAS

Silver Needles	140°F/60°C 8 minutes
Bai Mu Dan	140°F/60°C 6 minutes

CHINESE GREEN TEAS

Young Chinese green teas	158°F/70°C 4 minutes
Other Chinese green teas	158°F/70°C 3 minutes

JAPANESE GREEN TEAS

Gyokuro	122°F/50°C 1 minute
Sencha Ichibancha	158°F/70°C 2 minutes
Other Japanese green teas	176°F/80°C 3 minutes

OOLONGS

Western method	203°F/95°C 6 minutes
Gong Fu Cha method	203°F/95°C 20 to 60 seconds

BLACK TEAS

First flush India and Nepal	185°F/85°C 3 minutes, 45 seconds
Second and third flush India and Nepal	194°F/90°C 4 minutes
Other India teas	194°F/90°C 4 minutes
China, Sri Lanka, and other sources	194°F/90°C 4 minutes

DARK TEAS

Raw Pu Erhs	194°F/90°C 4 minutes
Black Pu Erhs	194°F/90°C 4 minutes

FLAVORED TEAS

Jasmine teas	158°F/70°C 3 minutes
Smoked teas	194°F/90°C 4 minutes
Flavored green teas	158°F/70°C 3 minutes
Flavored oolong teas	194°F/90°C 6 minutes
Flavored black teas	194°F/90°C 4 minutes

HOW MANY INFUSIONS?

*Traditions vary when it comes to the number of times tea leaves are infused.
In the West, there is usually just a single infusion, but tea leaves are used repeatedly in China
and Japan. The culture's relationship to tea and to time is revealed in these practices.*

IN JAPAN

Three successive, increasingly brief, infusions
draw out the three distinct flavors of tea:
sweetness (*gan*), bitterness (*ju*), and astringency
(*ku*). Each stage is distinct, meticulous, and precise.

IN CHINA

Very brief successive infusions—sometimes just
15 or 20 seconds for a grand cru—unfurl the leaves
like an unfolding narrative. The process of infusion
and tasting meld into a single symbiotic experience.

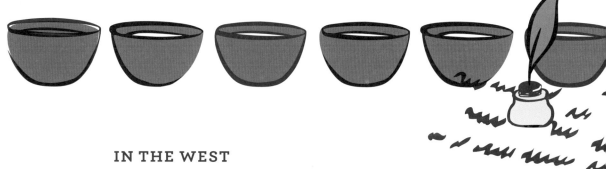

IN THE WEST

A single infusion reflects the the English style of
measuring out tea leaves. There are two distinct
moments in this ritual: preparation and tasting, a
"before" and an "after" the infusion.

SERVING TEMPERATURE

*It's an often-overlooked detail, but serving tea at the proper temperature is essential
for a successful tasting. It's foolish to burn your mouth rushing to drink a tea that will only improve
with a few minutes' cooling, enhancing the taster's experience.*

THE PERFECT TEMPERATURE

The ideal temperature for enjoying tea is between 104° and 122°F/40° and 50°C.

You can sip tea hot, warm, cool, or even iced, but don't drink it boiling hot or you'll scald your throat.

When the tea's temperature has dropped below 122°F/50°C, your lips will not retract upon contact with the liquor.

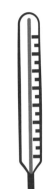

158°F/70°C: burning hot tea
140°F/60°C: excessively hot tea
122°F/50°C: the right temperature
104°F/40°C: lukewarm tea, intriguing
86°F/30°C: cool tea
64.4°F/18°C: iced tea

DIFFERENT MODES OF CONSUMPTION

✳ **Tea can be drunk hot:** this is the traditional method in most of the world.

✳ **Tea can be drunk warm:** from a culinary perspective, this is definitely the best approach, although it is not the most common way to serve tea. The mouth is not reflexively protecting itself from the liquor's extreme heat or cold, and you can therefore fully appreciate the tea's sensory profile.

✳ **It can be drunk cool** with a variety of foods at room temperature.

✳ **And then there's iced tea,** a beverage introduced in the United States.

USEFUL TIPS

✳ *To cool your tea, pour it back and forth between two cups. You'll decrease the temperature by about 18°F/10°C with each transfer.*

✳ *A kitchen thermometer allows you to precisely measure the temperature of your tea.*

✳ *If the tea is too hot, just take your time. Cradle the cup in both hands to warm your fingers. Anticipate the first sip, closing your eyes and indulging in a brief interlude of tranquility.*

PREPARING ICED TEA

Iced tea is a distinctive beverage in its own right. Healthier than sugary soda and more refreshing than water alone, it's an appealing, out-of-the-ordinary alternative to other soft drinks.

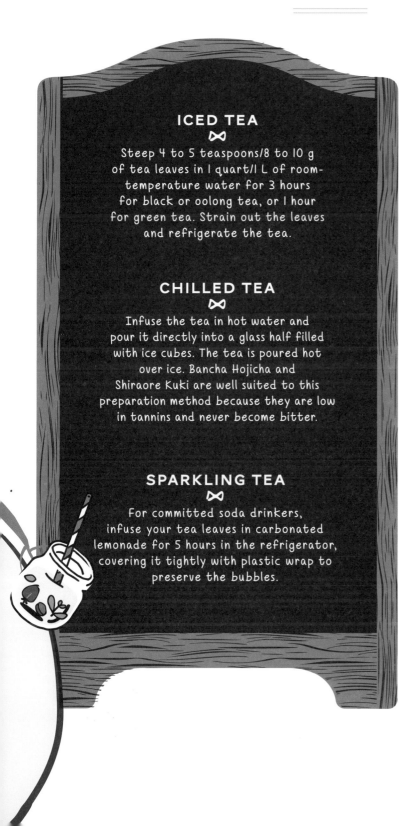

ICED TEA

⋈

Steep 4 to 5 teaspoons/8 to 10 g of tea leaves in 1 quart/1 L of room-temperature water for 3 hours for black or oolong tea, or 1 hour for green tea. Strain out the leaves and refrigerate the tea.

CHILLED TEA

⋈

Infuse the tea in hot water and pour it directly into a glass half filled with ice cubes. The tea is poured hot over ice. Bancha Hojicha and Shiraore Kuki are well suited to this preparation method because they are low in tannins and never become bitter.

SPARKLING TEA

⋈

For committed soda drinkers, infuse your tea leaves in carbonated lemonade for 5 hours in the refrigerator, covering it tightly with plastic wrap to preserve the bubbles.

THE CONCEPT

The leaves are infused in cold water. It's not a good idea to refrigerate hot tea because its tannins regroup and form an unpleasant film on the liquid's surface.

ICED AND FLAVORED

Flavored teas lend themselves to being served iced, especially those enhanced with red or citrus fruits. Serve them in a pitcher with cubed or shaved ice and fruit slices (apple slices, orange segments, or bunches of red currants, depending on what's in season).

SERVING TEA AT ROOM TEMPERATURE

Now that you've mastered hot and cold tea, try serving the beverage at room temperature, around 68°F/20°C. This is the perfect temperature when pairing tea with various foods.

SUBTLE PAIRINGS

Room-temperature tea works wonders when paired with cheeses or sipped with pastries.

The tea helps the food to dissolve in the mouth and release all its flavors. The beverage will be at a slightly higher temperature than the food, and cheese will dissolve more rapidly when combined in the mouth with warm saliva and tea.

THE RECIPE

Infuse the tea in cold water at room temperature for 1 hour for Japanese or Chinese green teas, and 3 hours for black teas from China, India, and Sri Lanka. For a Taiwan Oolong or a vintage Pu Erh, steep in the refrigerator for 3 hours.

DO YOU TAKE MILK, SUGAR, OR LEMON WITH YOUR TEA?

In many Western traditions, milk, sugar, and lemon invariably accompany a cup of tea. Although they may be acceptable additions in some cases, it's a mistake to use them when drinking fine teas.

GUIDELINES

* A great tea, like a great wine, should be enjoyed on its own with nothing added.

* A splash of milk in broken-leaf tea or an overbrewed cup reduces its bitterness.

* Sugar neutralizes the flavor of tea, but a pinch of sugar in a spiced variety may accent its taste, since sugar is a flavor enhancer. If you insist on a sweetener, use honey.

* Lemon kills tea. If you must, try a few drops of orange juice in a full-bodied black tea to add an unexpected hint of flavor.

CHOOSING A TEAPOT

Select the best utensils to get the maximum pleasure from your tea.
A true tea lover will have a dedicated teapot for each variety, and the cupboard will boast
as many teapots as tea selections.

GUIDELINES

✳ Use separate teapots for brewing individual tea varieties and flavored teas, because the essential oils used in their preparation can linger in the pot.

✳ Use a special teapot exclusively for smoked teas having powerful aromas.

✳ Avoid excessively large teapots (40-ounce/1.2 L or more).

✳ For good teas, use teapots with a maximum 10-ounce/300 ml capacity. For grands crus, you should use tasting sets. For Chinese teas, Gong Fu Cha or Zhong utensils are de rigueur.

SEASONED TEAPOTS

Unglazed ceramic teapots have a porous interior that absorbs minute tea particles. Tannins and other flavors gradually deposit a dark coating that affects the taste of future brews. These teapots are said to be "**seasoned**," and the deposit formed inside is called the "**memory**." Such teapots should be reserved exclusively for a single type of tea. Teapots **"without memory"** are fashioned from porcelain, cast iron, or glass. The material is inert and the teapots can be used for a variety of types of tea.

A MINI-TEAPOT WITH MAXIMUM FLAVOR

It's far easier to brew an excellent cup of tea in a smaller teapot (up to 20 ounces/600 ml) than in a larger one (1 quart/1 L or more). A small pot does justice to the delicate aromas of the tea because its contents are consumed more rapidly. If you keep your tea warm in a teapot, sipping it all morning long, the flavors will change for the worse and quality will diminish because its aromas evaporate. It's far better to prepare small quantities of tea in a little teapot throughout the morning.

CHOOSING A TEACUP

Just as the teapot is an essential tool for tea preparation, the teacup is the indispensable accessory for tea tasting. As it conveys the beverage to the mouth, the cup plays an active role in stimulating the senses, particularly when it touches the lips.

GUIDELINES

A teacup should be made of a material that is sufficiently thick and relatively inert so as not to conduct excessive heat.

The lips are actually far more sensitive to heat than is the interior of the mouth, and they experience a burning sensation at a lower temperature.

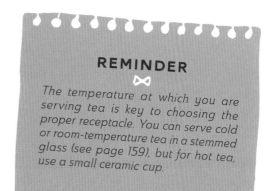

REMINDER

The temperature at which you are serving tea is key to choosing the proper receptacle. You can serve cold or room-temperature tea in a stemmed glass (see page 159), but for hot tea, use a small ceramic cup.

THE IDEAL CUP?

a porcelain cup
for any kind of tea

a glass cup
to enjoy the tea's color

an earthenware cup
to savor the subtleties of
your favorite variety

an infusing cup

a cup with a dark interior
to help you focus on the
aromas, suitable for
conducting a blind tasting

a stemmed glass
for serving a chilled tea
to surprise your guests

a mug
for the office

a generously sized cup
to warm your hands
by a cozy fireplace

TAKING CARE OF YOUR TEAPOT

Tea is a beverage that melds subtlety with aromatic richness. Tea utensils should have no lingering odors, however mild. Cleaning with soaps and detergents should be avoided.

GUIDELINES

✳ If you have a seasoned teapot (see page 28), never rinse it out. Just wipe the exterior.

✳ If you have a teapot "without a memory," rinse it out with clean water only.

✳ Never use dishwashing products, even to clean your teapot's exterior.

✳ Leave the teapot uncovered when you store it after cleaning, especially if you're not planning to use it for an extended period. This precaution will prevent odors from developing.

WASHING TEACUPS

✳ If you have seasoned teacups (see page 28) that retain tannins and aromas, do not rinse them—allow their patina to develop over time.

✳ If you have teacups "without a memory," simply rinse them in clean water.

✳ You can rub the outside of your cups with a **clean damp cloth** if necessary, but never use a dishwashing product.

ACCESSORIES FOR TEA

*Let's review the utensils that are indispensable—or discretionary—
when preparing an excellent cup of tea or organizing the ideal conditions for a tea tasting.*

AN ARRAY OF PRODUCTS FOR THE TEA LOVER

a spoon rest
for your strainer
after the infusion

a book that's essential
reading for every tea
lover who wants to
enhance the pleasures
of tea tasting!

an electric teakettle
with an adjustable
thermostat for water
that's always at the
perfect temperature

one (or more)
teapots

one (or more) teacups

canisters for storing
your favorite teas

a tea ball to dunk
into your mug at the
office when you don't
have a teapot handy

a timer to keep track
of the proper
infusion time

a tea scoop
for measuring

practical paper filters
that give the tea leaves
space to express their
personality

STORING YOUR TEA

Although tea is a dry product (the processed leaves have a maximum 3 to 4 percent moisture content), it is still a fresh, perishable substance.

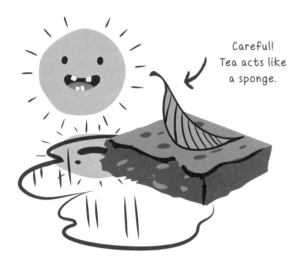

Careful! Tea acts like a sponge.

GUIDELINES

✳ Tea should be stored in an opaque, waterproof container. Air, heat, light, humidity, and odors—which tea leaves rapidly absorb—can cause a significant decline in quality.

✳ Tea has a particular aversion to air, particularly its oxygen content. Tea leaf components, including their flavor molecules, oxidize upon contact with air and continue to deteriorate with exposure.

✳ Tea is also averse to light and warm temperatures. Subjected to UV rays and heat, tea leaves dry out, losing their color and fragrance. It becomes impossible to infuse the tea properly; the leaves will crumble into dust at the lightest touch.

STORING DIFFERENT TYPES OF TEA

Appropriate storage times vary from one type of tea to another. **Generally speaking, teas characterized by floral, herbal, fresh, and iodized notes have shorter shelf lives than richer teas with woodsy, animal notes.** Many black and oolong teas retain their distinctive qualities for years. **Nevertheless, all teas, whatever their flavor profile, deteriorate with age, except for Pu Erhs (known as dark teas).**

Some teas are more perishable than others, including Ichibancha, first flush Darjeelings, and young green teas. Drink these when they're fresh for maximum enjoyment.

Pu Erh teas are stored in jars and are enhanced by aging, although there is still no consensus on the best conditions for doing so. Generally speaking, the same controlled temperature and humidity conditions recommended for storing cigars and wine are also appropriate for Pu Erh teas.

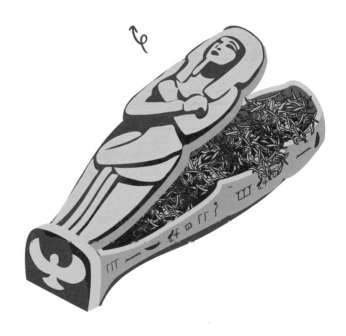

WHERE TO PURCHASE TEA

Purchasing tea should be a thoroughly pleasurable experience. Feel free to sniff the teas you are offered. If you don't have any specific requirements, tell the merchant about your tastes and preferences to receive expert professional guidance.

BASIC RULES FOR A GOOD TEA BOUTIQUE

✳ *Clients are encouraged to smell teas before purchase.*

✳ *The seller must be able to answer all your questions and give you advice, just like a wine merchant.*

✳ *Tea should not be stored or sold near coffee or spices; the confusion of odors will prevent you from fully appreciating the tea.*

✳ *Infusion times and water temperatures should be specified on the containers.*

✳ *If you don't have a tea boutique nearby, go ahead and order online. Make sure that a complete description of each tea (flavor profile, preparation method and use, distinctive qualities) is included.*

TASTING
TEA

WHY HOLD A TEA TASTING?

According to time-honored tradition, we refer to "taking tea" or simply drinking or sipping it. These terms reveal that tea is not really integrated into our culinary tradition, nor does it play a significant role in our daily lives and routines. Organizing a tea tasting requires us to direct our attention very specifically to sampling a tea. We cease to treat it as a mere convention, and recognize it as a distinctive beverage in its own right, whose riches deserve to be relished at leisure.

PREPARATION FOR A TEA TASTING

ensure the ideal conditions
for the tea tasting: a pleasant atmosphere,
ample time, tranquility, and focus

select a high-quality tea,
perhaps even a grand cru,
and give care to its
proper preparation

choose the right water
and heat it to the
perfect temperature

take note of
the fragrance and color
of the dry leaves

steep the tea
for the appropriate
period of time

carefully select
suitable utensils

observe the infused
leaves, the liquor's color,
its fragrances, and its
flavors before bringing it
to your lips

A BRIEF TOUR OF THE WORLD OF TEA TASTING

In the East, tea tasting is an ancient tradition, and tea is an integral part of daily life. But in the West, "taking tea" is primarily a social convention. These days, people all over the world are realizing that the vast array of tea varieties boast a myriad of flavors and fragrances.

In the West, we're discovering very rare teas to be savored like great wines.

In the East—in Japan, China, Taiwan, and India, in particular—there is growing awareness of the teas produced in neighboring countries. Until recently, interest has been limited to local production.

TEA IS SERVED!

Tea is increasingly earning acceptance in the culinary world. It is being accorded a place of honor on the tables and the menus in the world's most renowned restaurants and hotels. This growing recognition has given rise to the still novel profession of tea sommelier. Tea lovers are challenged to choose among a vast array of tea varieties. Some of these options are unfamiliar and difficult to understand. Aficionados seek advice and information on the teas themselves, as well as suggestions on successful pairings of teas with food.

AWAKENING ALL FIVE SENSES

Every tea tasting stimulates each of our five senses to varying degrees. Think of a tasting as a concatenation of micro-events, each engaging a particular sense. Two senses constitute what we superficially refer to as "taste," but all of them come into play during a tasting.

LISTEN, OBSERVE, SMELL, TASTE, TOUCH

✳ **We hear** the kettle come to a boil.

✳ **We observe** the dry leaves, the moistened leaves, and the liquor.

✳ **We smell** the fragrance of the dry leaves, then the scent of the leaves that have been infused.

✳ **We feel** the liquor's temperature at the initial contact with the lips.

✳ **We smell** the tea's aromas when we take the liquor into our mouth.

✳ **We are attentive** to the flavors of the tea perceived by the tongue.

✳ **We touch** the dry leaves, and take a moistened leaf in our fingers to unfurl it. When tea enters the mouth, we experience the sense of touch inside the cheeks and on the palate and tongue.

CON·CEN·TRATE!

The sense of sight influences our judgment and can be deceiving. An intensely colored liquor in the cup does not necessarily indicate a comparably flavorful brew. Similarly, the appearance of tea leaves with an abundance of lovely buds may give an erroneous impression that the tea will be delicious.

Sounds can be distracting. If your neighbor is loudly praising a tea during the tasting, you may be influenced to overestimate its quality and expect a grand cru. If someone comments on the aroma of ylang-ylang, you may find yourself becoming more conscious of floral notes than if you had enjoyed the tasting in silence.

When you are in the midst of a tasting, stay focused and avoid being distracted by conversations around you.

WHAT HAPPENS IN THE MOUTH

The act of tasting is a routine event that often goes unremarked upon when we eat.
But taste depends on a more complex set of mechanisms than you may realize that occur more or less
consciously. If you wish to appreciate the rich complexity of a tea, it's helpful to have a thorough
understanding of the role played by your mouth, nose, and other senses in the tasting process.

GUIDELINES

✳ If possible, breathe through your mouth, inhaling audibly.

✳ Hold the liquor in your mouth before swallowing.

✳ Swirl the liquor in your mouth to appreciate its texture and flavors.

✳ Breathe out gently through your nose to enhance your perception of the aromas.

THE ADVANTAGES OF PUTTING THOUGHTS INTO WORDS

The best way to remember smells is to name them. When you smell a tea's fragrances or aromas, try to define them objectively. Seek out the most advantageous tasting conditions, including silence. The evocative power of smell often defies objective description, and many scents conjure up deep-seated pleasurable or negative associations. We perceive these smells with great intensity.

OLFACTION AND RETRONASAL OLFACTION

What we generally (incorrectly) call "taste" is a phenomenon that involves flavors (taste sensations) and, even more important, smells (olfactory sensations). The "taste" of a tea is in fact primarily attributable to aromas. The olfactory substances contained in the leaves are perceived mostly through retronasal olfaction (our ability to smell food and drink as it passes through our mouth).

HOW IT WORKS

We smell tea in three distinct ways, listed here in ascending order of importance:

✳ Through direct olfaction: Position your nose above dry or moistened tea leaves, breathing normally.

✳ By sniffing the tea: Take short, sharp intakes of breath above the leaves you wish to smell.

✳ By retronasal olfaction: Take tea into your mouth and exhale air through your nose.

THE DIRECT ROUTE

Your first contact with tea is usually olfactory, when you breathe in.

Smell the dry leaves, then the moistened ones, sniffing the tea as you inhale.

The scent molecules will enter the nasal cavity through the nostrils, traveling across the nasal cavity and reaching the sensory zone where odors are perceived. This process is known as direct olfaction, but it conveys only limited information on what you're about to drink.

In fact, using this external path, your sensory zone perceives only 10 percent of the molecules that reach the area, because your nose has a protective mechanism that shields you from olfactory pollution and ambient air conditions.

To perceive more aromas, sniff the tea, inhaling quickly and repeatedly.

EXERCISES TO ENHANCE YOUR RETRONASAL OLFACTORY SKILLS

⋈

These simple exercises will help you differentiate between the sensations received through retronasal olfaction and those discerned in the mouth.

✳ Pinch your nostrils closed and take a sip of a favorite tea. Pay close attention when you swallow. You'll notice that your tea has no aroma and tastes dull. By blocking the nose, you've prevented retronasal olfaction from occurring and playing its role in revealing aromas.

✳ To enhance your retronasal olfactory perceptions, exhale deliberately and slowly while holding the tea in your mouth.

RETRONASAL OLFACTION

When the tea is held in your mouth, you experience the sensations of touch, heat, and flavor recognition. When you swallow, retronasal olfaction occurs: you exhale air through your nose, which then leads to an inhalation of air through your mouth. The "breeze" sweeps through the entire sensory zone for smell, and you'll therefore perceive 100 percent of the scent molecules.

To understand the importance of this process, just try blocking your nose when you swallow: retronasal olfaction is prevented and your perception is confined to the four flavors (sour, bitter, sweet, umami) that exist in tea.

It's actually the sense of smell that allows us to perceive most of the essential aromatic complexity of a beverage such as tea, which we call "taste."

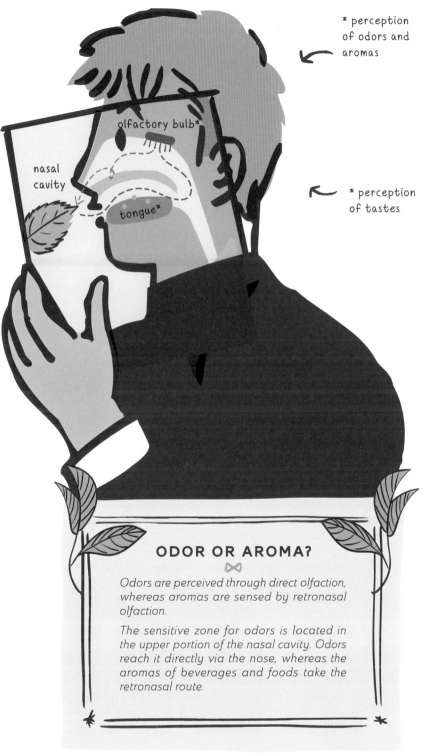

* perception of odors and aromas

* perception of tastes

olfactory bulb*

nasal cavity

tongue*

ODOR OR AROMA?

Odors are perceived through direct olfaction, whereas aromas are sensed by retronasal olfaction.

The sensitive zone for odors is located in the upper portion of the nasal cavity. Odors reach it directly via the nose, whereas the aromas of beverages and foods take the retronasal route.

TWO SUGGESTIONS
FOR ENHANCING OLFACTION

*Various regions of the world consume tea differently, and they have perfected utensils
that are ideally suited to their own methods of tea preparation and tasting. Gong Fu Cha and
specially designed tasting sets are two distinctive approaches to tasting that emphasize
the olfactory dimension of tea. They have inspired the design of accessories specifically created
to enhance teas' aromas.*

GONG FU CHA SMELLING AND TASTING CUPS

Gong Fu Cha is the traditional technique for preparing a variety of Chinese teas (see page 62). Every utensil is expressly designed to celebrate, express, and enhance a tea's distinctive bouquet.

A new accessory was created in the 1960s: a tall, narrow sniffing cup that captures the fragrance of the tea before it is poured into the smaller tasting cup. This invention has since been adopted as an essential tool in the tasting experience. It has become a central aspect of the art of tea, whose goal is to foster and enhance the experience of smell and taste.

TASTING SETS

Developed in England in the late nineteenth century and probably based upon a series of adaptations of Chinese Zhong practices (see page 61), a professional tasting set has three components: a bowl, a 4-ounce/120 ml cup with a serrated rim, and a cover. The cup and its cover are virtually hermetically sealed and designed especially to retain the fragrances from the infusion process. The taster can inhale the aromas by pouring the contents of the cup into the lid.

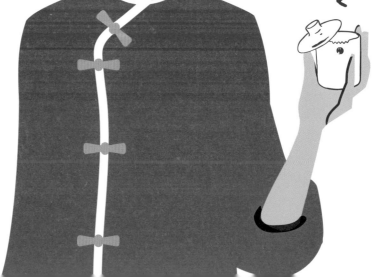

A MENU OF FLAVORS

Strictly speaking, taste is the sense that allows us to perceive flavors.
Four of the five flavors (sweet, salty, sour, bitter, and umami) are present in tea; the exception is salt,
which never occurs naturally in the beverage.

GUIDELINES

The tongue, the only organ of the body that has taste buds, is the primary means of perceiving flavors. Although they do not have strictly specialized functions, taste buds are susceptible to various flavors in differing degrees: you can actually create a sensorial map of the tongue.

Bitterness is not a flaw, except when it is overpowering and interferes with the tea's balance. We may not initially enjoy the taste, but it is part of the flavor profile of many tea varieties. Tea is classified as a bitter beverage.

Umami flavor occurs, often in minute quantities, in various Japanese teas, including Gyokuro and first flush Darjeelings produced from the AV2 cultivar.

An acidic taste is identifiable in certain black teas, including first flush Darjeelings, Qimen Mao Feng, and Assam teas.

acidic
bitter
acidic
umami
salty
salty
sweet

The flavor of salt is completely absent from tea, except among the Tibetans, who use it to season their brew!

Sweetness is present, often in infinitesimal quantities in Bancha Hojicha, Bai Hao Oolong, and Pu Erh teas. In China, sweetness is considered a measure of quality for Pu Erhs.

WHAT IS UMAMI?

Umami (which means "delicious" in Japanese) is the least familiar flavor for Westerners because it is not common-place in their cuisines. Although umami was first described in thirteenth-century Asian gastronomy writings, it was not formally classified until 1905. Very prevalent in the cuisines of Japan and China, this flavor comes from a combination of natural substances, including monosodium glutamate, an amino acid found in certain fatty fish (mackerel, sardines) and soy sauce, as well as in cheese, meat, and even breast milk.

THE AROMAS OF TEA

The aromatic palate of tea is as infinitely varied and rich as that of wine.
Naming and describing the perfumes of tea are intrinsic aspects of the pleasure we experience when
tasting the beverage. We usually proceed from the general to the particular in such descriptions,
from the olfactory family to the specific aroma.

∝ THE FRUIT FAMILY ∝

---------------------------- ORCHARD FRUITS ----------------------------

pear   apple   apricot   plum   cherry   mirabelle

peach   quince   Muscat grapes   green grapes

---------------------------- BERRIES ----------------------------

strawberry   raspberry   black currant   blackberry   red fruits   black fruits

...

CITRUS

bergamot   orange   grapefruit   lemon

TROPICAL FRUITS

mango   passion fruit   lychee   kiwi

COOKED AND DRIED FRUITS

prune   date   fruit preserves   fruit compotes   candied fruit   fig   raisins   cherry pits

NUTS

bitter almond   sweet almond   chestnut   walnut   sweet chestnut   hazelnut

...

⤬ THE GREEN AND HERBAL FAMILIES ⤬

------------------------------ FRESH PLANTS ------------------------------

green
sprouts

privet

sap

fresh-cut
grass

fennel

cress

mushrooms

sorrel

------------------------------ COOKED VEGETABLES ------------------------------

artichoke

zucchini

green
beans

spinach

------------------------------ DRIED PLANTS ------------------------------

wicker

straw

hay

tobacco

------------------------------ AROMATIC HERBS ------------------------------

mint

sage

thyme

cilantro

basil

anise

bay leaves

...

∝ THE WOODSY, EARTHY FAMILY ∝

---------------------------------- **EARTH** ----------------------------------

cellar

rocks

moist soil

rain-soaked
dirt after
a storm

wild
mushrooms

peat

saltpeter

---------------------------------- **WOODSY** ----------------------------------

resinous
wood

dry wood

sandalwood

balsam

cedar

vetiver

pine

burning
wood

boxwood

truffle

arnica

---------------------------------- **FOREST FLOOR** ----------------------------------

humus

damp
leaves

patchouli

moss

camphor

...

∝ THE FLORAL FAMILY ∾

----------- FRESH FLOWERS -----------

rose

orange blossom

hyacinth

geranium

peony

freesia

lilac

lily of the valley

----------- WHITE FLOWERS -----------

jasmine

daisy

mimosa

marguerite

wisteria

lily

osmanthus

----------- TROPICAL FLOWERS -----------

tiare flower

orchid

frangipani

magnolia

ylang-ylang

damask rose

∝ THE MINERAL FAMILY ∾

metal wire

hot metal

flint

burnt stone

...

⧓ THE FOOD FAMILY ⧓

-------------------------------- **DAIRY** --------------------------------

| fresh butter | melted butter | cream | milk | condensed milk |

-------------- **SWEET AND VANILLA FLAVORS** --------------

| vanilla sugar | pollen | honey | honeycomb | malt |

-------------------------- **SWEET TREATS** --------------------------

| chocolate | cocoa | marzipan | mocha | cream of chestnut | caramel | tarte Tatin |

------------------------------- **TOASTED** -------------------------------

| roasted coffee | toasted bread | bread crust | popcorn | brioche | peanuts | toasted nuts |

...

✂ THE SPICE FAMILY ✂

-------------------------- SWEET SPICES --------------------------

cinnamon   licorice   vanilla   anise   nutmeg

-------------------------- PIQUANT SPICES --------------------------

cloves   cardamom   pepper

✂ THE SMOKY FAMILY ✂

bacon   juniper   tar

✂ THE ANIMAL FAMILY ✂

stable   tack room   horse   musk   leather   sheep wool   wet wool   wild animals

...

∝ THE SEAFOOD FAMILY ∽

--------- SHELLFISH ---------

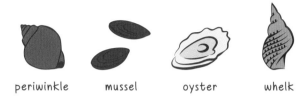

periwinkle   mussel   oyster   whelk

--------- CRUSTACEANS ---------

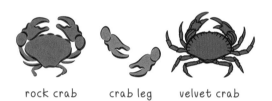

rock crab   crab leg   velvet crab

--------- FISH ---------

salmon   fish skin   raw fish   grilled fish
steak

--------- OTHER ---------

iodine   seaweed   kelp

...

TOUCH

Touch, the third sense that comes into play during a tasting, is an essential factor in assessing the texture of a tea. Its role in tasting may seem surprising, although the importance of touch is obvious when sampling foodstuffs. No matter what variety of tea you prepare, it is ultimately an aqueous solution with a consistent viscosity.

HEAT AND COLD

Mouthfeel (somatesthesia, for specialists in the field) is influenced first and foremost by the perception of heat and cold.

Water temperature plays a definitive role in tea preparation and is equally important in tasting. When the mouth comes into contact with an excessively hot liquid, the tissues contract to counteract discomfort and pain. We are so totally focused on this unpleasant sensation that our other senses effectively shut down.

Professional tasters always allow their tea to cool slightly, both to accentuate its characteristics and to maximize their olfactory and gustatory perceptions.

THE TEXTURES OF TEA

Although all teas have the same degree of viscosity, they provide very different textural effects based on the levels of polyphenols (also known as tannins; see page 57) they contain. When you taste a tea, these molecules create an impression of fullness, astringency, or even "density," depending on their size. In the realms of both tea and wine, astringency has the effect of constricting the mouth's buccal tissue as the tannins in the liquor create a puckering sensation.

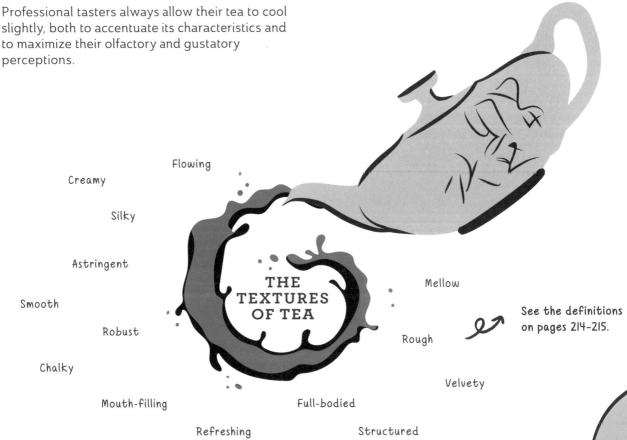

Flowing

Creamy

Silky

Astringent

Smooth

Robust

Chalky

Mouth-filling

Refreshing

Oily

THE TEXTURES OF TEA

Mellow

Rough

See the definitions on pages 214-215.

Velvety

Full-bodied

Structured

Dense

Round

SIGHT AND SOUND

In addition to providing information, the sense of sight influences expectations of what we are about to taste. The same applies to hearing. So, during tastings, we often try to confine these senses to a secondary role.

EVADE THE SNARES OF SIGHT

Before you even put a food in your mouth, you have a preconceived idea of how it will taste. But this notion creates an expectation that may distract you from your actual sensory perceptions, sometimes to the point of creating false impressions.

Tastings are often performed blind to avoid such influences. We frequently conceal information about the tea (its name, price, and grade), as well as the appearance of its leaves. For example, if you observe a tea with an abundance of buds, you may be tempted to conclude prematurely that its liquor will be delicious. And when the tasting is carried out in a group setting, it is preferable not to observe the smiles and grimaces of your neighbors.

THE BENEFITS OF SILENCE

Hearing also conveys a great deal of information, verbal and otherwise, that can bias our perceptions during a tasting.

A tasting should always begin with a period of silence so that all participants can concentrate on their individual sensations. If one person calls out certain perceived aromas, there's a strong likelihood that the other tasters will be inclined to search for the same flavor to the detriment of their individual perceptions. Both the experience of the tasting and the sharing of sensations will be diminished.

AROMATIC PROFILES AND HARMONY IN THE MOUTH

The many sensations (odors, aromas, tastes, textures) that we perceive in a tea combine to form what is known as its organoleptic, or "aromatic" profile.

A QUESTION OF BALANCE

A tea's organoleptic profile may be balanced or unbalanced, harmonious or discordant. An overly pronounced texture may spoil a distinctive aromatic bouquet, for example. An excessively strong taste may obscure a tea's evocative fragrance.

Harmony is essential for a satisfying, or even exceptional, tea. Harmony in the mouth is characterized by a succession of pleasing, well-balanced sensations that seamlessly follow one another, often culminating in an agreeably lingering aftertaste.

A sweet flavor makes this a very likable tea, extremely appealing from the initial attack. The aftertaste is rich and complex, with sustained fruity, spicy, and woodsy notes...

Full and balanced; the aromas linger in the mouth long after the last sip...

Following the "attack" (initial taste sensation), the notes develop very gently. A delicate tea, with a complex, lasting finish in the mouth...

DESCRIBING A TEA'S AROMATIC PROFILE

A few examples from tasting notes...

Mellow and complex, lingering in the mouth and developing like an aged wine whose notes form a remarkably harmonious sequence...

Soft, delicate, and very powerful. A tea of great character, presence, and intensity, with a lingering aftertaste. Dominant notes are complemented by an abundance of subtle nuances that contribute to the tea's richness...

A BRIEF LESSON IN MOLECULAR SCIENCE

When subjected to the action of water and heat, the components present in tea leaves migrate into the water, passing into the "aqueous phase." Depending on the duration of the contact and the water's temperature, these elements dissolve more or less completely and in varying amounts.

CARBOHYDRATES

Although tea leaves contain considerable quantities of carbohydrates, just one of them is soluble and only in tiny quantities: **monosaccharide**. It is responsible for the very subtle sweetness apparent in certain teas.

(presence in the tea leaf: about 25%)

POLYPHENOLS

Polyphenols (also known as **tannins**) are in the same category as those found in wine.

(presence in the tea leaf: about 30%)

MINERALS AND VITAMINS

Fresh tea leaves are naturally rich in **vitamin C**, but the nutrient is completely destroyed when the leaves are subjected to high temperatures during the roasting or drying process. Tea also contains **vitamins B and flavonoids**, along with **fluoride**, **potassium**, **calcium**, and **magnesium**.

(presence in the tea leaf: about 3%)

AMINO ACIDS

Tea contains about twenty of these substances. **Theonine**, the most prominent among them, occurs only in tea and constitutes about 60 percent of tea's amino acids.

(presence in the tea leaf: about 15%)

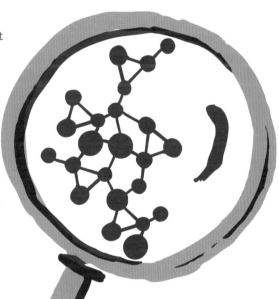

AROMATIC AND FRAGRANT COMPONENTS

These are the substances that give tea its bouquet and are its "soul." A tea may contain up to six hundred of these!

(presence in the tea leaf: about 0.1%)

XANTHINES

Tea contains three naturally occurring varieties of nitrogenous molecules: **caffeine**, **theophylline**, and **theobromine**. Caffeine is the most significant of these.

(presence in the tea leaf: about 3%)

THEINE AND CAFFEINE

Caffeine is the primary alkaloid in tea. First discovered in coffee in 1819, it was isolated in tea a few years later and named theine *before scientists realized that they were both the same molecule.*

A STIMULATING BEVERAGE

Although the caffeine that occurs in tea is identical to the molecule in coffee, it has noticeably different effects. Caffeine diffuses into the bloodstream very quickly when you drink a cup of coffee, reaching the brain in less than 5 minutes. This generates the well-known coffee "rush," whose effects dissipate in 2 to 3 hours.

The caffeine contained in tea is coated with polyphenols, and these molecules are released gradually over a period of up to 10 hours. Tea provides long-term stimulation. This is why caffeine in tea is classified as a mild stimulant, while that in coffee is considered to be more powerful.

IT'S EASY TO DECAFFEINATE TEA

Brew your tea for 30 seconds and empty out this first infusion. When you prepare a second infusion, 80 percent of the theine will have been eliminated.

But avoid decaffeinating a grand cru or a very aromatic tea because the procedure diminishes some of its bouquet. The longer tea is infused in hot water, the more caffeine dissolves. On the other hand, a tea infused for 1 hour at room temperature will be extremely low in theine.

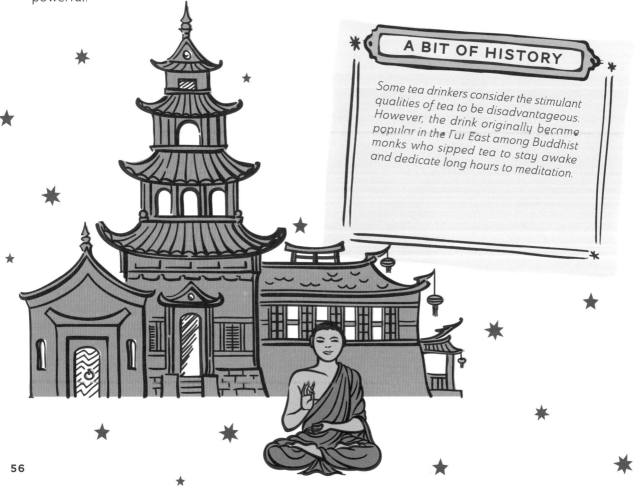

A BIT OF HISTORY

Some tea drinkers consider the stimulant qualities of tea to be disadvantageous. However, the drink originally became popular in the Far East among Buddhist monks who sipped tea to stay awake and dedicate long hours to meditation.

TANNINS IN TEA

Polyphenols are also referred to as tannins. They belong to the same family of components that are contained in wine, although some of them, including epigallocatechin gallate, occur only in tea.

OVERVIEW

Tea's tannins, or polyphenols, consist primarily of catechins. As oxidation occurs, a portion of the catechins are converted to two other molecules, thearubigin and theaflavin, which give oxidized teas their reddish to brownish color.

WHAT DO THEY DO?

Certain tannins or polyphenols are responsible for the texture of a tea. It is their presence that produces mouthfeel: the sense of astringency, puckery sensation, and perception of the liquor's body or density. A number of tannins develop a bitter taste. These components are released gradually during the brewing process.

The buds and the first leaves of a tea branch are richer in polyphenols than are the leaves lower down on the plant. This is one reason that a high-quality harvest includes only the buds and the upper leaves of the plant.

HEALTH NOTE

⋈

Scientific research focuses on the health benefits of tea (see pages 98–99).

TEA TASTING WITH FRIENDS

Tasting tea with friends gives you an opportunity to enhance your understanding of the drink while exploring a range of teas in good company. Think of it as a grown-up parlor game. Tea tasting focuses on the sense of smell, which we sometimes neglect, and encourages participants to awaken and pay attention to their olfactory perceptions.

EQUIPMENT

* a teakettle with an adjustable thermostat

* a tasting set for each tea

HOW TO PROCEED

* The host prepares the selected teas and brews them.

* Without speaking, the guests study and smell the dry leaves;

* then they examine the infused leaves and sniff them;

* then they observe the liquor's color and clarity;

* and, finally, they take a sip and analyze its texture, flavors, and aromas through retronasal olfaction (see pages 40–41). This entire phase should be carried out in silence while noting down impressions.

When everyone has finished, resume the tasting, beginning by examining the dry leaves. This time, discuss your impressions and enjoy sharing your experiences with the other participants.

TASTING NOTES

Noting your impressions during a tea tasting helps you articulate your reactions, and naming them more precisely helps you define them. As you repeat this very entertaining exercise, you'll be amazed by your progress—maybe with practice you'll become a tea sommelier yourself one day!

• INFORMATION •

Tea name

Origin

Color

Infusion time

Water temperature

Other information

• DRY LEAVES •

Appearance

Color

Aromas

• INFUSION •

Appearance

Color

Aromas

• LIQUOR •

Color

Mouthfeel

Flavors

Aromas

Aftertaste and organoleptic profile

You can download a tasting note form from
www.ecoleduthe.com/fichedegustation.pdf.

TASTING SETS

A tasting set is an essential tool for professionals. It is uniquely valuable in revealing all facets of a tea because it allows a remarkable degree of control over all aspects of the infusion process. Tasting sets can be adapted to any type of tea.

A BRIEF LESSON ON TASTING SETS

1. Arrange all the samples you intend to taste in front of you and compare them.

2. Get out as many sets as you have teas to taste.

3. Place 1 teaspoon/2 g of tea leaves in each set.

4. Pour in about 3.5 ounces/100 ml of water heated to the proper temperature and let it steep for the appropriate amount of time.

5. When the infusion is complete, pour the liquor into the bowl, keeping the cover on the cup to retain the leaves and prevent them from getting into the liquor.

6. The tea will now be present in three stages—the dry leaf, the infused leaf (which is called the infusion), and the liquor. It is time to begin the tasting.

For the dry leaf and the infusion (the leaves that have been infused), assess:

✳ **appearance:** the leaves' size, color, quality of the harvest, presentation

✳ **texture:** the leaves' pliability or resistance, degree of saturation of the dry leaf

✳ **fragrance:** the dry and infused notes

For the liquor, pay particular attention to the:

✳ **color and clarity** of the liquid

✳ **mouthfeel and tactile sensations**

✳ **flavors and aromas**

✳ **aromatic profile**

4-ounce/120 ml cup with serrated rim

pouring cover

bowl

TASTING WITH A ZHONG

The Zhong, also known as a gaiwan *(covered bowl), is a very delicate,
handleless porcelain cup with a lid and a saucer. In Chinese homes and teahouses,
it is the vessel most commonly used for preparing white and green teas.*

A BRIEF LESSON ON THE ZHONG

1. Just as you would for Gong Fu Cha (see page 62), always rinse the Zhong with hot water before using to clean and warm it.

2. Depending on the volume of leaves, fill the Zhong with leaves to a quarter to half of its capacity. This proportion may be lowered for denser varieties of tea (Long Jing, Jasmine Pearls, etc.).

3. Pour about a quarter Zhong's worth of cold water over the leaves to moisten and prepare them for the hot water, then top up with water heated to just below the boiling point.

4. This first liquid is immediately poured out into a bowl or onto a tea tray. Its purpose was to rinse the leaves and partially open them, facilitating the release of aromas during the second infusion.

5. You can now smell the leaves infused directly in the Zhong, as well as various fragrances from the tea that cling to the inside of the lid.

6. Prepare the second infusion following the same procedure as for the first: a base of cold water followed by filling the cup with hot water. You can use varying infusion times, depending on individual preferences.

7. The lid allows you to swirl the leaves to control the intensity of the infusion and block them within the cup when you are tasting the tea. By slightly lifting the lid, you can taste tea directly from the Zhong. It is interesting and instructive to sniff the inside of the lid repeatedly, because the fragrances evolve during the successive infusions.

THE GONG FU CHA TASTING METHOD

*Gong Fu Cha can be translated as "infusing tea systematically and diligently"
or simply as "leisure tea." It is the traditional Chinese method for preparing oolong and Pu Erh teas.
The teapots used for Gong Fu Cha often surprise Westerners by their small capacity,
which rarely exceeds 3.5 to 5 ounces/100 to 150 ml; however, they are ideally suited to the
multiple successive infusions practiced in the ancient Chinese art of tea tasting.*

sniffing cup

teapot

tea scoop

reserve teapot

tasting cup

tea tongs

tea tray

ceremonial linen cloth

A BRIEF LESSON ON GONG FU CHA

1. First arrange the utensils on a tea tray.

2. Heat water in a large kettle that has a capacity several times that of the teapot. When the water comes to a simmer, fill the teapot, which has been set out on the tray. It is essential to warm up the teapot because it is so small that the quantity of water needed for the infusion process cools very quickly. Empty the teapot into the reserve teapot.

3. Fill the teapot a third to half full with tea leaves and pour in a little water to rinse the leaves. Immediately empty out this first infusion, which has simply been used to moisten the leaves, into the reserve teapot or into the cups to warm them up.

4. Empty the cups and the reserve teapot and drain them on the tea tray.

5. Fill the teapot again to the brim, allowing the water to overflow and eliminate any foam.

6. This first infusion is completed within 30 seconds. Then, empty out the contents of the teapot into the reserve teapot to the very last drop.

7. Pour the liquor into the sniffing cup and transfer it immediately to the tasting cup.

8. Smell the sniffing cup; although it is empty, you will sense the fragrances of the tea.

9. Taste the tea in the second cup slowly, in little sips. With the best teas, you can repeat the infusion of the same leaves ten times, following the same procedure.

STEP 3

STEP 5

STEP 6

STEP 7

STEP 8

TASTING MATCHA TEA

Matcha is the tea used in the Japanese tea ceremony known as Cha No Yu.
Unlike all other types of tea, it is whipped, not infused. This "mousse of liquid jade" is prepared
using a whisk in a bowl rather than a teapot. Invigorating and intense, Matcha is
usually served with very sweet food; the contrast complements the tea's subtle bitterness.

A BRIEF LESSON ON MATCHA

The preparation of Matcha is part of a rigorously codified ritual that is one of the principal paths followed in the practice of Zen Buddhism. But you can also drink it for sheer pleasure!

1. Preheat the bowl: fill the bowl about a third full with hot water, and soak the whisk (*chasen*) in it. Once the bowl is heated, discard the water, then dry the bowl with a clean cloth (an optional step).

2. Measure out 2 teaspoons of Matcha (about 1 g) with a bamboo spoon and pour it into the bowl. You can sift the powder to prevent lumps.

3. Pour about 2.5 ounces/ 70 ml of hot water (149° to 158°F/65° to 70°C) over the powder in the bowl.

4. Holding the bowl in your hand, whisk vigorously in a zigzag motion, whipping the mixture until you have an emulsified mousse. When the Matcha is foamy, it's ready to drink.

CHA NO YU

In Japan, the act of drinking tea has implications that go beyond reverence for a traditional way of life and aesthetic sensibilities. The practice has assumed a philosophical dimension. Cha No Yu (literally "hot water for tea") is practiced following a meticulously coded ritual.

This ceremony developed in the late fifteenth century and was formalized in the sixteenth century by Sen no Rikyū. The ritual is performed in an austerely designed pavilion reserved for the purpose, following rigorous rules of etiquette. The tea ceremony has played a defining role in Japanese architecture and landscape design. It has also profoundly influenced the society's code of conduct and remains a key element in the understanding of Japanese culture.

KYUSU TASTING

*The Kyusu is a small Japanese earthenware or porcelain teapot with a
hollow handle on one side. It is equipped with a strainer that prevents the tea leaves from escaping.
This pot is traditionally used for green tea. The most common size is 12 ounces/360 ml,
but for the finest teas, capacity is limited to 3.5 to 7 ounces/100 to 200 ml.*

A BRIEF LESSON ON KYUSU

1. Organize the equipment: a Kyusu teapot with three bowls, a container of tea leaves, and a measuring scoop.

2. Heat the water in a kettle to just below the boiling point.

3. Place the tea leaves in the pot.

4. Fill two of the three bowls with hot water if you are preparing a Sencha, or just one of the three if you are making a Gyokuro.

5. Using the third empty bowl, cool down the water by pouring it from bowl to bowl as described on page 24.

6. When the water has reached the desired temperature, pour the contents of the bowls over the leaves in the teapot.

7. When the infusion is complete, pour the contents of the teapot into the three bowls, distributing the tea evenly among them because the last few drops are the most concentrated.

8. Repeat the process, following the same procedures but shortening the infusion time by a third for each subsequent infusion.

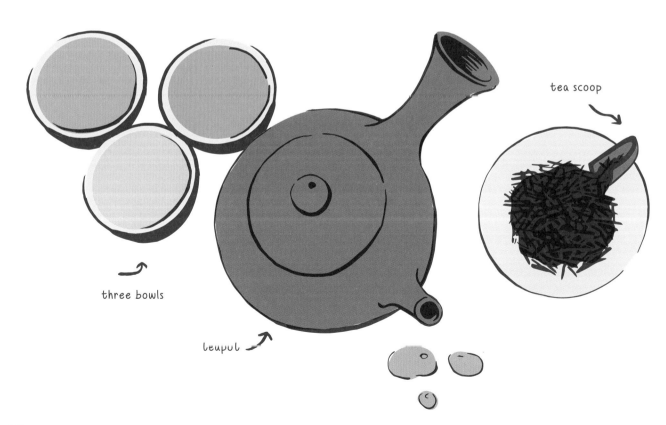

tea scoop

three bowls

teapot

66

EXPLORE TEA BIT BY BIT

As you begin to explore the world of tea, it is advisable to follow a gradual process that will lead you from teas with powerful aromas to increasingly subtle varieties. You'll find they vary in the sensation they create in the mouth, their texture, and their olfactory impact.

A GRADUAL INITIATION

As you progress in your discovery of tea, start with strongly structured teas that have pronounced aromas. Then, pursue your explorations with teas that are increasingly subtle in terms of mouthfeel, texture, and olfactory properties.

white teas

green teas

oolongs

black teas

flavored teas

A TASTING ITINERARY

For example, you might begin with simple black teas and culminate with Chinese grands crus, progressing through green and white teas, oolongs, and Pu Erhs.

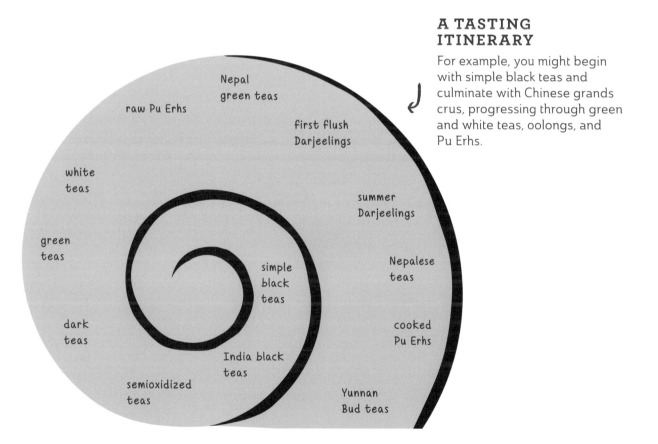

Nepal green teas

raw Pu Erhs

first flush Darjeelings

white teas

summer Darjeelings

green teas

simple black teas

Nepalese teas

dark teas

cooked Pu Erhs

India black teas

semioxidized teas

Yunnan Bud teas

WHAT IS TEA?

THE TEA PLANT IS A CAMELLIA

*The tea plant (*Camellia sinensis *or* Thea sinensis, *"Chinese camellia") is a shrub in the large family of* Theaceae. *It is related to the camellias that grow in our gardens and includes three principal varieties. The first originated in China and is known as* sinensis; *its leaves are small and olive green in color. Another variety,* assamica, *comes from Assam and has broad, light, fleshier foliage. A third, less common variety,* cambodiensis, *has been found in Cambodia but is not cultivated.*

A BRIEF LESSON IN BOTANY

The three varieties of *Camellia sinensis* have given rise to numerous hybrids, some naturally occurring and others are the fruit of human intervention. **Today, there are more than 500 different types of tea plant**, known as cultivars, developed from these three types, each with its own distinctive characteristics.

The domestic tea plant is a shrub 3 to 6 feet/1 to 2 m high, depending on the variety. Some wild tea plants are centuries old and as much as 100 feet/30 m tall. The tea plant's evergreen leaves have a shiny upper surface and an inner surface that is matte and a lighter shade of green. The young leaves and buds ("pekoe," from the Chinese *pak-ho,* "fine hair" or "down") have a fine silvery-white coating.

The tea flower is white with five petals. It sometimes appears singly on a branch or in a bunch of three or four blossoms. The fruit of the tea plant is a round seed with a hard shell, measuring from 3/16 to 5/8 inch/4 to 15 mm.

A BIT OF HISTORY

It is thought that tea was discovered in China around 2700 BC. A legend relates that Shen Nong, a mythical Chinese hero, had commanded his subjects to consume only water that had been boiled, for health reasons. It happened that a few tea leaves fell into the boiling water, and one taste sufficed to persuade everyone of the virtues of this fragrant beverage. There is evidence that tea was being consumed in China by the eighth century BC. The first Westerners to learn of tea's existence were the missionaries and great explorers of the sixteenth century, but it was not until the seventeenth century that Dutch merchants introduced tea to a broad European audience.

TEA "VARIETALS"

*Certain grape varietals are used to make specific wines. Similarly, some types of tea
are better suited to the production of green tea, and others to black. In viticulture,
there is a tradition of acclimating grape varieties to growing conditions far from their place of origin.
This practice has given rise to a remarkable degree of globalization in the wine business.
In contrast, cultivation of individual tea "varietals" is often confined to a limited geographic zone.*

THE END OF REGIONALISM?

The regional nature of tea cultivation is
primarily due to limited communication among
the world's tea-growing regions. Tea growers
have demonstrated limited interest, and even
indifference, to developments elsewhere, and
this attitude has discouraged experimentation.
However, a few pioneers in Nepal and some
African countries are beginning to successfully
introduce Chinese and Japanese cultivars to
their plantations.

WHAT'S A CULTIVAR?

The term cultivar comes from
the contraction of the term
"cultivated variety." It results
from selection, hybridization
(the crossbreeding of two species or genera), or spontaneous mutations in the plants.

A FEW REPRESENTATIVE "VARIETALS"

Yabukita
Japanese growers value this cultivar for its
tolerance of low temperatures and its herbal,
iodized fragrance. This variety constitutes 85
percent of the tea planted in Japan. It is easily
recognized by the shape of its long leaves,
which grow upward toward the sun.

Da Ye ("large leaves")
It is used to make Pu Erh teas in China and is one
of the most strongly scented cultivars. When fresh,
its leaves have a fragrance reminiscent of a freesia
bouquet. Dried, they develop a strong animal
scent with leather and stable notes.

AV2 (Ambari Vegetative 2)
Cultivated in various tea-growing regions of India
over the last twenty years, this varietal yields
outstanding results in the organoleptic properties
of its teas, particularly Darjeelings. It offers an
unparalleled lively floral bouquet.

TTES12 (Taiwanese Tea Experiment Station
no 12 or Jin Xuan)
Taiwan uses this variety to make various Dong Ding
teas. With its very intense notes of butter and sweet
spices, sometimes accompanied by pronounced
ylang-ylang floral notes, it makes remarkable teas
that are reminiscent of vanilla-flavored milk.

TERROIRS

The tea plant's ability to adapt to very diverse soils and geographic conditions invites comparison with viticultural growing practices. It raises questions on the influence of terroir on the sensory properties of any given tea.

DO TEAS HAVE TERROIRS?

There's no doubt that the physicochemical composition of soil has an influence on tea plants, but it is difficult to determine to what extent it affects the character of a particular tea. This uncertainty is attributable to the regional fragmentation that prevails among tea-growing countries. It is rare for growers to take an interest in what their neighbors are doing in other regions, far less in other countries. Cultivars are therefore markedly differentiated by region. There are very few examples of a tea plant being acclimated from one terroir to another, so it is difficult to establish comparisons between the same cultivar grown following the same practices but in different soils.

It should be noted that the role of terroir in wine and tea production is perceived quite differently. For wines, the issue of terroir is a firmly established aspect in the quest for quality. In contrast, most tea drinkers are not habituated to considering terroir, and its influence on any particular tea is not recognized as a significant issue.

WHAT IS TERROIR?

Terroir *signifies an area of land with environmental features that are physically homogeneous and distinctive, cultivated with certain traditional techniques, and lending itself to the production of various agricultural products.*

FERMENTATION OR OXIDATION?

Freshly plucked leaves can be made into teas of any color: green, black, blue-green (oolong), white, dark, or yellow. The process that produces this variety of colors is referred to as fermentation in tea-producing circles. However, the process involved is actually oxidation, not fermentation.

THE PRINCIPLE

Oxidation is a natural phenomenon that causes any harvested plant to fade and oxidize (its pigments begin to turn brown, for example).

When processing tea, controlling its oxidation determines the tea's color as well as most of its gustatory properties.

Fermentation of Pu Erhs under cover (see page 83)

HOW IT WORKS

The tea leaf's cells contain an enzyme known as oxidase. When these cells are broken—whether naturally, by damage to the leaf's cellular structure, or deliberately by rolling—this enzyme is released and begins its oxidizing action.

Reacting with the oxygen in the air, the enzyme oxidizes and converts the polyphenols present in the leaf, metabolizing the catechins into two other groups of molecules, the thearubigins and the theaflavins, which are primarily responsible for the liquor's color.

✳ **For black teas**, the oxidation process is completed and the leaf is 100% oxidized.

✳ **For semioxidized teas**, known as oolongs, the process of oxidation is interrupted and the leaf is oxidized 10%, 20%, 30%, or up to 70%.

✳ **For green teas**, the oxidation process is eliminated.

✳ Finally, a Chinese family of teas known as **dark teas** actually undergoes a genuine process of fermentation (see pages 82–83). These are the only teas that benefit from aging.

HOW TO MAKE A GREEN TEA

*The processing of green tea was long considered a uniquely Chinese prerogative.
But Japan now produces green teas exclusively, and some of them rival Chinese production in quality.
More recently, other tea-producing countries (including the northern regions of India) have
experimented with green teas, but they have not yet achieved impressive results.*

ANCESTRAL TECHNIQUES

Local expertise and ancestral tradition vary among regions and sometimes even among neighboring villages. These artisanal practices produce teas of outstanding quality with aromatic finesse, pleasingly presented leaves, and delicious liquors.

THE PROCESSING OF GREEN TEAS

Green teas are not oxidized. The processing method may vary considerably depending on the country, region, or local expertise. However, the process includes three steps that are taken to prevent oxidation, and these are the same everywhere.

1. Roasting

This process kills the enzymes that cause oxidation in the leaves. To accomplish this, the leaves are heated very rapidly to about 212°F/100°C in large pans (the Chinese method) or by steam (the Japanese method) for between 30 seconds and 5 minutes. This makes the leaves soft and pliable for rolling.

2. Rolling

The leaves are then fashioned into the form of a small stick, ball, coil, or even a tea leaf, in the case of a Long Jing, for example. This step may be carried out using a cold or hot process, depending on the quality of the harvest.

Young shoots can be easily rolled cold because they contain a great deal of moisture, unlike more mature leaves that have to be rolled immediately after roasting while they are still hot.

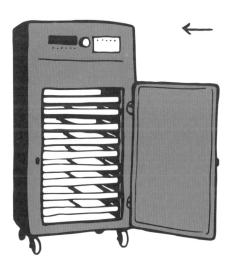

3. Firing

The leaves now require a more rigorous dehydration process, which is essential to preserving the tea. They are spread out on racks where warm air is circulated for 2 to 3 minutes. They are then allowed to rest for 30 minutes. The process is then repeated until the moisture content of the leaves is no more than 5 to 6 percent.

4. Sorting and packaging

Finally, the leaves are sorted before being packaged.

HOW TO MAKE AN OOLONG

When making oolong teas, oxidation is halted partway through the processing.
More mature leaves, which contain fewer tannins and less caffeine, are often used for this type of tea.
Oolongs are a specialty of Fujian, a coastal province in southwest China, and Taiwan.

THE TWO PRINCIPAL TYPES OF OOLONG

There are two principal categories of oolong teas.

✳ **lightly oxidized teas** (10%–15% oxidation) prepared using the so-called Chinese method

✳ **teas in which oxidation is considerably greater** (60%–70%), processed using a method developed more specifically in Taiwan. The processing of semioxidized teas is actually not clear-cut. Each plantation has its own recipes and produces teas whose oxidation percentage does not necessarily correspond to these two categories. Whatever the case, all semioxidized teas must undergo the following stages of processing.

THE PROCESSING OF OOLONG TEAS

1. Withering

The leaves are left to wither in the sun for several hours, then cooled in the shade. This procedure, which tenderizes the leaves, is repeated two times. The oxidation process begins.

↓

2. Sweating

This is the most important step in the production of semioxidized teas. In a room that is maintained at a temperature between 72° and 77°F/22° and 25°C with a humidity level around 85 percent, the leaves are continually stirred with ever-increasing force. This process frees the aromas from the leaves and facilitates water evaporation. The degree of oxidation in the final product depends on the length of this stage.

In the so-called Chinese method, sweating is halted when the leaves are about 10 to 12 percent oxidized. These teas are light with leafy flavors.

In the so-called Taiwanese method, the sweating process is longer, allowing oxidation to reach up to 70 percent. This process produces teas that are fruitier and darker.

During sweating, the leaves may be stirred and tossed in various ways, which also contributes to the creation of a very distinctive tea.

3. Roasting

Once the desired degree of oxidation is reached, the leaves are roasted to halt the enzyme reaction that causes oxidation. This process is similar to the way green tea is processed (see pages 74–75).

4. Rolling

At this stage, the leaf is shaped into the desired form, in the same way as green teas are. The leaves are often very large and may be just creased or sometimes rolled into large pearls, as in the case of Dong Ding tea.

5. Drying and packaging

Finally, the leaves are dried and packaged.

HOW TO MAKE A BLACK TEA

Black teas, known as "red teas" in China for the coppery red hues of their infusions, are fully oxidized.

THE PROCESSING OF BLACK TEAS

1. Withering

Withering gives the leaves a pliable consistency that allows them to be rolled at a later stage of processing. The fresh leaves lose half of their water content during withering. The harvest is spread out evenly on stacked racks in a room where the temperature is maintained between 68° and 75°F/20° and 24°C, and the air is circulated using fans. This process usually takes between 18 and 32 hours.

2. Rolling

The rolling process for black tea differs from that of green tea; in this case, the objective is not to shape the leaf; rather, to break down the cell walls to facilitate the enzyme reactions of oxidation. When lightly rolled, the leaves produce a mild tea, and when more vigorously rolled, a fuller-bodied one. Rolling may be done mechanically or by hand, and this stage takes 30 minutes. The process is sometimes resumed after the buds, which are tender and prone to breakage, are removed.

3. Oxidation

The rolled leaves are then sent to the oxidation chamber. The humidity in these rooms ranges from 90 to 95 percent, and the temperature is between 68° and 72°F/20° and 22°C. Good ventilation is essential, but drafts must be avoided. The oxidation process may take from 1 to 3 hours, depending on the quality of the leaves, the season, the region, and the desired color of the tea.

A BIT OF HISTORY

It is said that a ship laden with Chinese tea arrived in London in the seventeenth century after a particularly lengthy voyage. The tea had oxidized in the shipping crates during the journey, and the green tea had turned black. The English found the tea to be very much to their taste and soon ordered another shipment.

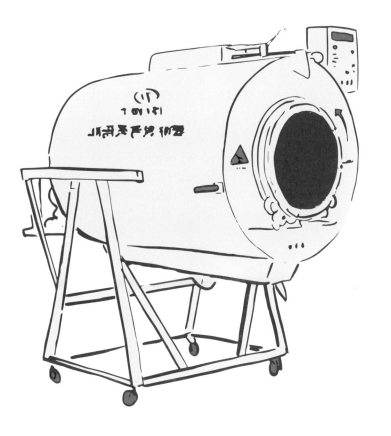

4. Drying

To halt oxidation, the tea must be heated as rapidly as possible to a high temperature. This drying process normally occurs in ovens where the leaves are subjected to 194°F/90°C heat for 15 to 20 minutes. At the conclusion of this process, the tea's moisture content should be 4 to 5 percent, because a totally dehydrated tea cannot be successfully infused.

5. Sorting and packaging

The tea is then sorted into whole and broken grades. Whether carried out by machine or using handheld screens, the sorting must be done quickly to prevent the tea from absorbing moisture. After sorting, the tea is packaged.

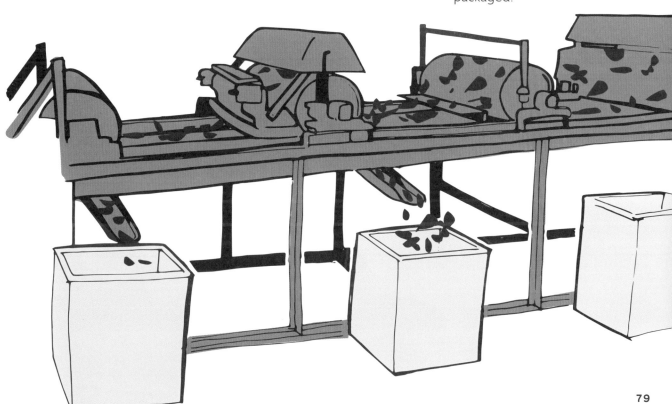

HOW TO MAKE A WHITE TEA

White teas are traditionally the specialty of the coastal province of Fujian, located in southwestern China. They are processed using the simplest means of all, but the procedure requires great finesse.

THE TWO PRINCIPAL TYPES OF WHITE TEA

✳ **Silver tip teas** consist exclusively of long, silvery buds.

✳ **Bai Mu Dans** consist of a sprig with a bud and two (or sometimes three or four) leaves.

THE PROCESSING OF WHITE TEA

Harvesting (of the bud and the two leaves beneath it) occurs just as the bud begins to open. White teas consist of leaves that are left in their natural state, undergoing only the following two processes.

1. Withering

Traditionally, withering occurred in the open air; the grower's expertise was needed to anticipate climatic conditions and to time the harvest accordingly. To better control these conditions, withering is increasingly carried out in temperature-controlled rooms (between 86° and 90°F/30° and 32°C) with sophisticated ventilation systems. During this step, oxidation begins, but since the leaf is not manipulated in any way, the process is extremely slow.

2. Drying

After withering in the heated chamber, the leaves lose all but 5 to 7 percent of their moisture. However, the prevailing humidity in Fujian at this time of year raises this percentage to 15 percent in just seconds. Therefore, the leaves must be subjected to a more intensive drying process, spread on shelves or trays in a hot air dryer.

3. Sorting and packaging

The leaves are then sorted by hand and packaged.

THE COLORS OF CHINESE TEA

*Most countries confine their tea color classifications to green, black,
and oolong categories, but the Chinese have their own descriptive system.
It is distinct from international criteria and is based on the color of the infused liquor.*

Classification of Chinese tea varieties is based on six families: green teas, blue-green teas, red teas, black teas, yellow teas, and white teas. The system reflects the diversity of Chinese teas and China's expertise in controlling the oxidation process.

Each color is the result of a very distinctive processing method, during which the tea leaf undergoes a greater or lesser degree of oxidation, giving each tea its tasting characteristics.

Chinese **green and white teas** are similar to those described in pages 74–75 and 80, but this is not the case for other varieties.

Blue-green teas are known as oolongs, whereas red teas are more commonly referred to as black teas in China.

Note that **Chinese black teas** should not be confused with those mentioned above. Instead, they correspond to what are described as "dark teas" in the West.

Yellow teas are very rare and similar to green teas in the way they are prepared.

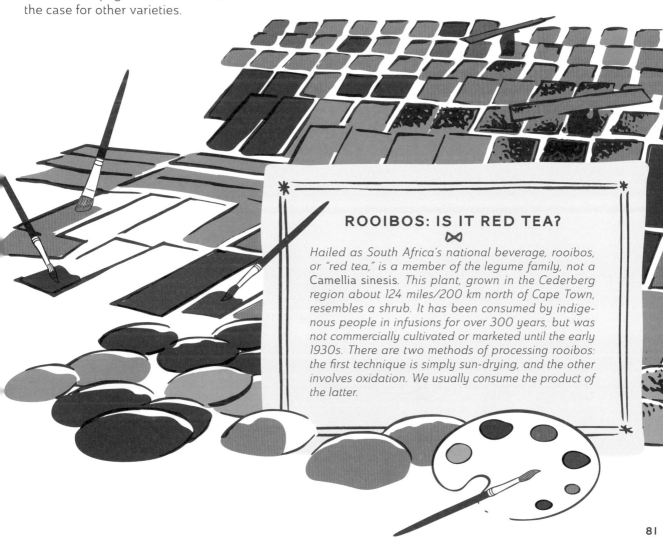

ROOIBOS: IS IT RED TEA?

Hailed as South Africa's national beverage, rooibos, or "red tea," is a member of the legume family, not a Camellia sinesis. This plant, grown in the Cederberg region about 124 miles/200 km north of Cape Town, resembles a shrub. It has been consumed by indigenous people in infusions for over 300 years, but was not commercially cultivated or marketed until the early 1930s. There are two methods of processing rooibos: the first technique is simply sun-drying, and the other involves oxidation. We usually consume the product of the latter.

HOW TO MAKE A DARK TEA

*Dark teas get their name from the deep brown color of their infusions.
Most dark teas come from Yunnan, a province in southwestern China, but Vietnam, Laos, and
Malawi also produce them. The best-known dark teas are the Pu Erhs, which are produced
exclusively in Yunnan from the Da Ye ("large leaves") tea varieties that are native to this region.*

THE TWO TYPES OF DARK TEA

In contrast to every other type of tea, the harvest and preparation of leaves for dark teas occur in different times and places. At the conclusion of two very different processes, the same leaves will produce two distinct types of dark tea.

٭ Green, or raw, teas
(*sheng* in Chinese) are often compressed and ferment naturally over a period of years. This is the traditional process, dating back 3,000 years in China, and represents the most ancient method of transporting tea, pressed into bricks or cakes.

٭ Black, or cooked, dark teas
(*shu* in Chinese) are sold in bulk or compressed. Their fermentation is accelerated by human intervention.

The initial processing steps are the same for both types.

THE FIRST STEPS

1. Drying in the sun

The harvested leaves are spread out in the sun for about 24 hours. The heat has the effect of drying out the leaves and destroying the enzyme responsible for oxidation. Oxidation actually does occur, but to a very limited extent. This step is very important for the tea's fragrance.

2. Storage

Once the leaves are dried, they are stored before being sold to large manufacturers or Pu Erh dealers. The mode of manufacture selected determines which type of Pu Erh is produced.

COMPRESSION OF GREEN TEAS

The leaves are compressed into various forms, including cakes, bird's nests, and bricks. During this process, the leaves are steamed, softened, and shaped in molds.

The compressed tea is then stored for aging by market intermediaries who purchase the tea in large quantities.

This postoxidation aging occurs due to the effects of microorganisms that are present in the tea. When fermentation is carried out under the proper conditions, storage allows the slow, natural fermentation of the tea leaves, whose organoleptic features develop with aging. Over a period of years, the naturally fermenting cakes turn into dark teas.

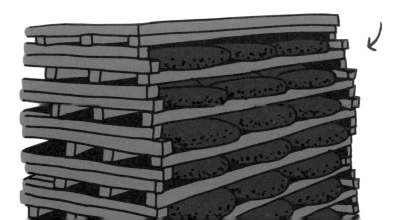

THE FERMENTATION OF COOKED DARK TEAS

These are teas whose fermentation process is initiated and accelerated by human intervention. The dry leaves are spread out in a thick layer, often on the ground, in rooms where the heat and humidity are strictly controlled. They are generously sprinkled with water and covered with a cloth or a tarpaulin. The temperature in the interior of the piled leaves quickly reaches 140°F/ 60°C. As the process begins under the combined effects of heat and humidity, microorganisms proliferate and wilt the leaves. This stage takes between 45 days and 3 months, depending on the degree of fermentation desired. This process ultimately creates the distinctive color of the leaves, ranging from brown to black, and the diverse array of aromas that characterize the dark tea family.

Sorting and compressing cooked dark teas

The dried leaves to be sold in bulk are passed through a screening device and sorted into various grades. Most of the leaves are compressed into cakes, bricks, or bird's nests.

The process for cooked dark teas was originally intended to accelerate the aging process for cakes of green tea. However, the process gives these teas organoleptic properties that differ considerably from those of naturally dried dark teas.

HOW TO MAKE A YELLOW TEA

On occasion, certain Chinese teas are presented as "yellow teas." Does this term suggest that there is actually another tea color?

THE PROCESSING OF YELLOW TEAS

There is a very small family of so-called yellow teas, whose characteristics place them somewhere between white and green teas.

The best-known yellow tea in China is Jan Shan Yin Zen, whose leaves undergo light fermentation during drying. In contrast to white tea, which is dried in the open air, yellow tea is dried on a light cloth.

A LITTLE HISTORY

Rather than referring to a particular style of fermentation, the adjective **yellow** *usually indicates a white or green tea of such exceptional quality that it is worthy of the emperor: yellow was the iconic imperial color. Each of the Chinese provinces was compelled to pay the emperor tribute in kind, and they reserved the best of their output for this purpose, whether they offered foods or other regional products. The tea-producing provinces did not escape this obligation, and they selected their very finest harvests for the court. Imperial tea thus became "yellow tea" by simple word association. These days, if you offer your guest a cup of yellow tea, consider yourself to be a host of distinction.*

HOW TO MAKE A SMOKED TEA

Smoked teas are black teas that owe their invention and distinctive qualities to a happy accident.

THE PROCESSING OF SMOKED TEAS

When smoked teas are prepared today, the initial processing is identical to the method used for making traditional black teas (see pages 78–79). But after being rolled, the leaves are lightly toasted in a heated iron pan and then spread out on bamboo shelves over a fire fueled by pinewood. The length of this process is determined by the degree of smokiness desired.

A LITTLE HISTORY

The providential creation of these black teas occurred around 1820 in the Fujian region in southeastern China. The Chinese army requisitioned a tea plantation to use as barracks for its soldiers. Before handing over possession of his drying room, the planter desperately sought a way to dry the still-moist tea leaves and avoid losing the harvest. He started a fire with spruce wood and laid the leaves in a pan above it. The leaves rapidly dried, taking on a very distinctive smoky flavor. A few days later, a foreign trader visiting the planter happened upon this batch of tea, which no one knew how to use. Delighted by the flavor, he took it back with him to Europe, where it was enthusiastically received.

PREPARING TEA LEAVES FOR EVERY TASTE

The first Westerners to study tea believed that black and green teas came from different plants. Indeed, the Chinese, who maintained a monopoly in supplying tea to the West, jealously guarded the secrets of its cultivation and processing and were quite happy to foster the misapprehension.

ONE PLANT, MANY TEAS

Just a single plant, the *Camellia sinensis*, is the source of the vast and diverse array of teas throughout the world. Once harvested, the plant's leaves undergo many different kinds of processing and treatments.

The single most important of these processes is oxidation (see page 73). As the grower initiates and controls the process of oxidation, he determines and assigns the tea's color. Fresh tea leaves contain varietal aromas that differ from one cultivar to another. Some of them are precursors of the aromas that remain in the finished product. They may also alter during the processing of the tea, giving rise to new aromatic components.

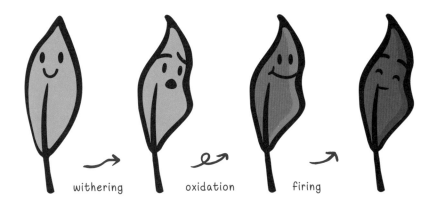

withering   oxidation   firing

THE FORMATION OF VARIOUS AROMATIC COMPONENTS

These components appear at different stages of the tea-preparation process. Many of them appear **during withering**, including those responsible for more or less herbaceous green notes or fresh floral fragrances (jasmine or hyacinth).

During oxidation, fruity (baked apple) and floral (violet) notes appear, as well as spicy fragrances (cinnamon, vanilla).

The prolonged contact of the leaves with a burning hot metal surface **during firing or drying** converts the proteins and sugars that are present in the leaves through the Maillard reaction. This produces toasted, caramelized scents and the aromas of toasted bread or nuts (chestnuts, hazelnuts).

In the postfermentation stage of some teas, animal, woodsy, and mushroom notes emerge.

SPRING HARVESTS

The tea plant's growth rate slows in the winter months, and during this period of dormancy, the young sprouts have the opportunity to build up essential oils much more intensively than at other times of the year.

THE DELICATE FIRST FLOWER OF HARVESTS

The first harvest of the year in springtime is particularly aromatic and therefore highly prized.

This is particularly true **in China**, where the finest green teas are made exclusively with the buds and first leaves of the spring harvest, which occurs in April in a number of provinces, including Zhejiang, Anhui, and Fujian.

These are known as **first flush teas**.

In India, the most renowned springtime harvest occurs in Darjeeling. The quality of these first-harvested leaves of the year depends on the preceding winter's weather patterns, which are highly unpredictable in this part of the world. Depending on these conditions, the harvest begins between the last days of February and the third week of March and continues until mid-May. There are also springtime harvests in Assam, but these are less frequent.

In Japan, Ichibancha (the "first harvest") is the most highly prized of the year for green teas. This crop is doubly valued by the Japanese, who ascribe symbolic import to every event associated with the change of seasons in their country.

GRADES OF TEA

In India and in all the other countries that currently produce black teas for the British market, the packaging frequently bears a series of letters that indicate the grade of the tea, if you know how to decipher them.

WHO DECIDES THE GRADE?

The leaves of green and semioxidized teas are generally whole, and their grade is not indicated on their packaging. The same holds true for a number of black teas, mostly Chinese, whose name is sufficiently respected to vouch for their quality. The grade is important, however, for other black teas because it indicates two characteristics:

✱ **the type of harvest** (greater or lesser quality)

✱ **the size of the leaf** (whole, broken, crushed)

DECIPHERING THE CODE

The word **orange** has nothing to do with the citrus fruit when used in grading. It signifies "royal," referring to Holland's House of Orange-Nassau. The term **pekoe** (from the Chinese **pak-ho**, "down" or "fine hair"), describes the bud, which has a silvery white down when it has not yet completely opened.

WHOLE LEAVES

FOP (Flowery Orange Pekoe) This is the finest harvest, consisting of the terminal bud and the two topmost leaves. The tea contains an abundance of buds known as "golden tips," which turn gold in the oxidation process.

INDIAN GRADES

In northern India, the description of the harvest is more detailed and gives a much more accurate indication of quality than is the case elsewhere.

GFOP (Golden Flowery Orange Pekoe): FOP with a large proportion of buds.

TGFOP (Tippy Golden Flowery Orange Pekoe): FOP containing many gold buds.

FTGFOP (Finest Tippy Golden Flowery Orange Pekoe): FOP of outstanding quality.

SFTGFOP (Special Finest Tippy Golden Flowery Orange Pekoe): FOP of truly extraordinary quality. The grade is usually reserved for the best first flush Darjeelings. The more letters (T, F, S) appear to the left of the designation, the more exceptional the harvest. A figure is sometimes added at the end of the grade to rate the gustatory quality of the tea itself, rather than the high quality of the harvest.

OP (Orange Pekoe)
Young, well-rolled leaves. Excellent harvest, but a bit later than in an FOP. Here, the terminal bud has already turned into a leaf.

P (Pekoe)
A leaf that is less fine and, after processing, longer than an OP. It does not contain buds.

S (Souchong)
A low, broad leaf that is older and much lower in theine content, often rolled lengthwise and used primarily for smoked teas.

BROKEN LEAVES

The leaf is no longer whole and is much smaller than in OPs. When brewed, the liquor is much more full-bodied and darker.

BOP (Broken Orange Pekoe)

FBOP (Flowery Broken Orange Pekoe)

GBOP (Golden Broken Orange Pekoe)

TGBOP (Tippy Golden Broken Orange Pekoe)

CRUSHED LEAVES

F (Fanning)
Flat pieces smaller than Broken. The liquor is very strong and deeply colored.

Dust
Leaves that are even more thoroughly crushed. The grade is used only in teabags.

CTC
This is not a grade, strictly speaking, but rather a process for converting tea leaves by Crushing-Tearing-Curling. The term clearly indicates the quality of the resulting product. Used almost exclusively for teabags.

Whole leaves

Broken leaves

Crushed leaves

WHAT IS A "VINTAGE" TEA?

Unlike wine, tea does not age well, and most types do not retain their gustatory qualities when stored. Dark teas are the exception to this rule, however, and are the only type that improves with age.

SHOULD TEAS CARRY A DATE?

Dating is essential in the case of cakes of green tea (see page 82), which must age for a minimum of 5 years before consumption. The aging process allows the tea's aromatic bouquet to develop, while mellowing its tannins and diminishing its astringency.

Cooked dark teas, on the other hand, can be consumed immediately because their aromas appear during the processing. However, a several-year storage period enhances the aromatic palate of the tea, bringing heightened complexity to its aromas.

It is therefore possible to speak of a vintage for this type of tea, but only in the restricted sense of dating the age of the tea. It never grades the climatic conditions that prevailed in a region during the year of the harvest, as is the case for wine.

THE SPECIAL CASE OF TAIWAN...

The concept of a vintage does apply to some teas produced in Taiwan. The island pays particular care to preserving its grand cru teas for very long periods of time. Due to the island's climate, these stored teas tend to absorb a great deal of moisture.

In response to these conditions, the Taiwanese developed the practice of roasting the stored leaves every 2 or 3 years. Certain specialized Taiwanese tea merchants offer teas that may be dozens of years old. The teas that are subjected to these repeated roastings develop some extremely interesting tasting notes over time.

WHAT IS A GRAND CRU?

Both wine and tea lay claim to their own grands crus, or remarkable products of a specific terroir. These tea harvests are more often than not produced by local artisanal growers who are unrecognized by westerners. However, they are revered by experts in the gastronomy of the country or region where they live.

THE MASTER ARTISAN

A grand cru owes its character to the dedicated artisan who creates it. The character of a harvest is admittedly influenced by the tea variety, the terroir, and the climatic conditions, but the most important aspect is the expertise and talent of its producer.

He controls every step, from cultivating the plant to timing the harvest and processing the leaves.

As a tea master, the artisanal producer studies the distinctive features of the leaves in the harvest. He assures that the best of these qualities are expressed during the leaves' processing. Every harvest is unique, and the details of the process are never the same from year to year.

TRADITION OR INNOVATION?

There are two main types of grand cru growers. One group subscribes to traditional practices, and the other might be termed "taste explorers."

Numerous regions in the tea-growing world perpetuate a sense of tradition and expertise that have been perfected over time, sometimes over centuries:

✳ **in China**, in the Zhejiang, Yunnan, and Anhui regions

✳ **on the island of Taiwan**

✳ **in Japan**, in the Shizuoka, Kyoto, and Kagoshima prefectures

✳ **in India**, at Darjeeling and in Assam

A grand cru may also be created outside established tradition. In regions that lack a strong heritage based on a particular variety of tea, small growers are establishing and devoting themselves to the exploration of all the gastronomic nuances that tea provides.

Currently, successful efforts are being made in various countries, including **Nepal**, to develop new tea varieties, work with different cultivars, and adapt alternative withering and rolling practices.

WHAT IS A BLEND?

The very finest teas are never blended, but most of the teas found in your cup are combinations of several different varieties.

THE ORIGINS OF BLENDING

Specialized professionals known as blenders offer up their nose and palate to dedicate themselves to creating product consistency. This is a métier of the utmost importance in the world of tea, from a strictly economic point of view. The profession began in the 1890s, when tea first became a product available for mass consumption. Faced with this new demand, tea manufacturers realized the importance of standardizing their products as well as securing their sources of supply.

THE BLENDER'S MISSION

✳ The blender's primary objective is to assure year-round consistency in the organoleptic properties of his product.

To provide regular consumers a tea that offers reliable, constant standards in terms of flavor and aroma, as well as appearance, agribusiness companies commit to providing clients with a standard, homogeneous, and consistent product.

✳ The second objective is to avoid any potential ill effects or mishaps arising from weather, political instability, or other unforeseen events on the tea production cycle.

When a tea begins to have an important economic role, it is imperative to eliminate these potential risks by combining several (sometimes as many as 70) teas into a given blend. In the event of a bad harvest or sharp increase in the price of one of these teas, only a tiny percentage of the final product will be affected. The impact on the breakeven cost and on the taste will be minimal. Thus, the blender's métier, which does indeed demand great skill and experience on the taster's part, is most often applied to fairly commonplace teas and the tea bag industry, with the notable exception of the great teas of China and Japan.

FLAVORED TEAS

*Flowers, fruits, and spices are sometimes used to enhance teas,
as in the case of Indian chai, for example. But any tea—whether green, black, or semioxidized—
can be flavored with various substances.*

AUTHORIZED SUBSTANCES

Substances that are authorized for flavoring tea are precisely stipulated by law. Most flavored teas primarily use flavors that are called natural or "identical to natural."

✳ Natural flavors

These are components derived strictly from natural ingredients. These include essential oils, extracts, and concentrates, and are obtained by extracting the aromatic substances that are present in spices, citrus rinds, or flowers. They are more rarely derived from fruits because their high water content does not facilitate the extraction process. Natural flavors often include a large number of different molecules, which contribute to the richness of the flavor.

✳ "Identical to natural" or synthetic flavors

These are flavors that exist in a natural state, but which are synthetically produced, often for economic reasons. They are sometimes referred to as synthetic flavors. From a molecular point of view, these flavors are absolutely identical to those present in nature, but they are often limited to the single note that predominates in the natural flavor.

✳ Artificial flavors

These flavors are actually quite rare in tea, contrary to widespread misconceptions. They are produced by a manufacturing process and do not exist in nature. They often resemble the molecules of a natural aroma, modified to augment their flavoring impact.

PERFUMED TEAS

*Tea readily absorbs other flavors, desirable and otherwise,
and great care must be taken to store it properly. The practice of flavoring teas is a tradition
almost as ancient as tea drinking itself.*

FLAVORING INGREDIENTS

Without going into inordinate detail on the earliest methods of tea preparation in China, it should be recalled that tea leaves were originally treated more as an ingredient to be included in a savory dish than as a refined beverage (see page 172). Until the end of the Tang Dynasty (618–907), tea was primarily regarded as a nutrient. Combined with butter, flour, onions, and spices, it was an ingredient in *tsampa*, an invigorating dish that continues to be a mainstay in the basic diet of the inhabitants of the Tibetan plateau.

A FLAVOR SPONGE

The practice of flavoring tea with the petals and pistils of freshly cut flowers apparently began during the Song Dynasty (960–1279). Rose, magnolia, chrysanthemum, lotus flowers, and, of course, jasmine were the most popular. With its ability to absorb any fragrance, tea proved to be an ideal vehicle for conveying other aromas in addition to its own. Eventually, growers began to add spices, bits of dried fruit, and herbs. Depending on their properties, these additions could be temporarily placed in contact with the tea leaves or mixed in with the final blended product.

Perfumed tea took on new prominence in the 1960s. Following the Second World War, the agribusiness sector revolutionized its business, creating flavorings and acquiring the technical ability to introduce them into foods. Tea was the perfect medium to make use of these new, predominantly fruity flavor notes that hitherto had been so hard to capture.

Experimenting with these flavors, combining them harmoniously with the right tea, each with its own fragrances, and ultimately creating a well-flavored product requires talent, expertise, and inspiration. In addition to a quality harvest and mastery of the complex oxidation process, the creation of these teas demands a perfumer's expertise.

MINT TEA: A SPECIAL CASE

Mint tea first appeared in the 1860s. Confronting the loss of the Russian market due to the outbreak of the Crimean War, the British turned to the North African ports of Mogador and Tangier to sell their tea cargos. At the time, infusions of mint leaves and absinthe were the most popular drinks in the Maghreb. The idea of combining mint with tea gradually took hold, and this new blend became increasingly popular.

SPICED CHAI

Masala Chai (recipe on page 97) is such an intrinsic part of life in India that many have the impression it has been consumed there since time immemorial. However, it only dates back to the nineteenth century. The British had chosen India as the United Kingdom's tea plantation, but 150 years later, the colony was consuming 80 percent of its own tea crop, having adopted and adapted English practices of adding milk and sugar, as well as its native spices. Cardamom is the basis of all Masalas, with the addition of other ingredients, including pepper, cinnamon, ginger, mace, and cloves.

A LITTLE HISTORY

A legendary tea known as Earl Grey first appeared in Europe around 1830. The story goes that during a diplomatic expedition in China, Charles, the Second Earl Grey and British prime minister, was given a very old recipe for tea flavored with bergamot from the hands of the emperor himself. Returning home, the earl offered the recipe to one of the two great London tea firms, who have each since claimed to have been the one he gave it to. The true story is quite different. Charles Grey never traveled to China. When he added a few drops of essence of bergamot to his tea to suit his own personal taste, he had no inkling that he would give his name to one of the most celebrated teas in history!

THE SECRETS OF JASMINE TEA

The Chinese practice of flavoring teas with petals of freshly cut flowers, natural oils, or fruit rinds has an ancient tradition. Producers use roses, magnolias, chrysanthemums, and, of course, jasmine, the most popular of all. The varying characteristics of these teas depend on the tea that is used as a base, as well as the care and patience devoted to the blending process.

THE JASMINE HARVEST

The best of the leaves destined to be made into green tea, which is the base for jasmine tea, are harvested during the month of April and processed as described in pages 74–75. The tea is then stored until August, when jasmine is harvested.

The best jasmine is gathered in the midafternoon, when the flowers are still closed but are just beginning to open as twilight begins. The harvest is left to rest for 3 or 4 hours while the flowers open completely and their temperature drops.

A BLEND OF LEAVES AND FLOWERS

The initial blending of dry tea leaves and flowers is carried out by spreading four to five layers, each 4 to 6 inches/10 to 15 cm thick. The tea leaves and the flowers are left in contact for about 12 hours. The blend is moved around to lower the interior temperature of the layers to about 97°F/37°C.

For the highest-quality jasmine teas, this process may be repeated up to seven times, with the addition of fresh flowers on each occasion. For example, the processing of 220 pounds/100 kg of one of the highest grades of jasmine teas (Yin Hao or Grand Jasmine Mao Feng) requires a total of 617 pounds/280 kg of fresh flowers. The process of putting them in contact with the tea leaves is repeated seven separate times.

THE SEPARATION OF THE LEAVES AND FLOWERS AND THE DRYING OF THE FLOWERS

For the finest jasmine teas, the flowers are removed by hand, one by one, to prevent them from adding any bitterness to the infusion. These flowers still retain some fragrance and are used to flavor additional jasmine tea blends of lesser quality. On occasion, the flowers are left in the tea or sometimes sold separately.

DELICIOUS CHAI

The British introduced tea to India in the early nineteenth century, and wild teas were discovered in Assam at the same time. Tea was originally produced for the British market, but it gradually became a very popular beverage in Indian society as a whole. These days, certain social elites continue to prepare their tea in accordance with the strictures of British ritual, but most Indians enjoy a daily brew that combines black tea, spices, and sugar infused in hot whole milk—the beverage known as chai.

THE SPICES IN CHAI

Each region and household has its own preferred blend of spices for making chai. Cardamom, cinnamon, ginger, cloves, pepper, mace, and nutmeg are among the most favored.

Indian chai is renowned for its soothing and warming qualities. It is also good for the digestion and conveys an astonishing sense of well-being. It's hard to say no to a second cup!

CHAI WALLAHS

These tea hawkers are everywhere you go in India—you'll find them on every street corner, every square, as well as on trains and all means of public transport. When you're waiting for your train to depart, one of these tea sellers might pass you a cup of chai through the open window of your carriage. The small earthenware cup (called a kullarh) has a scent that enhances the flavor of its contents; it is sometimes tossed to the ground and broken following use. What if the train starts to pull away before you've had a chance to pay the vendor? No worries, he'll find a way to clamber into the carriage and demand his due.

MASALA CHAI

Makes 17 ounces/500 ml, serving 5

In a pot, combine 8.5 ounces/250 ml each of water and milk with 5 teaspoons/10 g of black tea, 3 tablespoons of sugar, 2 cinnamon sticks, 2 whole cloves, 1 teaspoon of grated fresh ginger, a pinch of ground black pepper, a pinch of grated nutmeg, and 2 cardamom seeds. Bring to a boil and simmer, stirring, for 5 minutes. Strain and pour into small glasses. Serve very hot.

THE BENEFITS OF TEA

From its earliest days, tea has been considered a product that is beneficial to the body, with numerous medicinal properties. When ground into a paste, it has even been used in poultices to treat rheumatism.

SCIENCE AND SUPERSTITION

The many legends of tea, whether originating in China, India, or Japan, tout all of its stimulating and invigorating properties.

As the Chinese emperor Shen Nong, the father of Chinese medicine and agriculture, stated in his *Treatise on Plants*, tea "relieves fatigue, strengthens the ill, pleases the soul, and delights the eye."

Twentieth-century scientific research has enabled us to analyze the numerous benefits observed by tea drinkers for over 3,000 years.

Here's a brief summary of various components of tea and their health benefits:

XANTHINES

Caffeine is the most significant xanthine. It is present in tea in varying concentrations depending on how the tea is grown and processed. The caffeine level in buds is much higher than what is present in the plant's lower leaves. It is a powerful stimulant for the nervous system and allows tea drinkers to stay alert and focused, without experiencing jitteriness. This makes tea the ideal drink to support both physical and mental functioning. It is also known for its diuretic properties.

Theophylline is present in tea to a much lesser extent. It acts as a vasodilator, dilating blood vessels and improving blood flow. Vasodilatation is one of the processes that contribute to the regulation of the body's temperature. This is one reason that tea, whether drunk boiling hot or iced, is such a refreshing beverage.

Theobromine is a powerful diuretic. By stimulating renal processes, it facilitates elimination via the urinary tract.

TANNINS AND POLYPHENOLS

Catechins and **flavonoids** are the primary polyphenols in tea. Research on green tea has revealed their effect on the human body. The emphasis on green tea reflects the fact that most of these scientific studies have been carried out in Japan, a country that produces green tea exclusively.

Research shows that **polyphenols** in green tea have a desirable impact on bad cholesterol. Daily consumption of five cups of green tea produces a drop in bad cholesterol levels within a few months. Other studies have produced evidence of the effect of green tea in preventing cardiovascular disease, particularly arteriosclerosis.

Many scientific hypotheses on the effects of the antioxidant properties of polyphenols have also been tested. One of these, epigallocatechin gallate, has been studied with particular attention because it inhibits the action of the enzyme urokinase, which is responsible for the uncontrolled multiplication of tumor cells. Currently, research on this topic is being carried out on animals. The same results remain to be demonstrated in human subjects, but an effort is being made to establish a link between tea consumption and the prevention of certain cancers. None of these research projects have been carried out in a therapeutic environment as yet—instead they focus on a preventative healthy diet.

VITAMINS AND MINERALS

The tea plant is naturally rich in **vitamin C**, but this nutrient is completely destroyed when it is steeped in water that is over 86°F/30°C.

Tea consumption therefore does not contribute vitamin C to the diet. However, **flavonoids** are abundant in tea. They contribute to the general good health of the body, encouraging metabolic activity; that is, the entire range of physiochemical reactions occurring in human tissue (energy expenditure, nutrition, absorption).

Tea contains 0.3 mg of **fluorine** per cup. We must consume 1 mg of fluoride daily to protect our tooth enamel, so regular tea consumption makes a significant contribution to this requirement. In addition, the fluoride associated with the tannins in tea inhibits the formation of dental plaque.

THE WORLD'S TEA PLANTATIONS

WHERE TEA THRIVES

Tea plants flourish in warm, humid areas, ideally with rainfall that is consistent throughout the year.
Tea is cultivated between the latitudes of 42°N and 31°S.

IDEAL NATURAL CONDITIONS

The optimal average temperature for tea growing is between 64.5° and 68°F/18° and 20°C, but there may be significant fluctuations, particularly at night. **Climate** influences both the volume and the quality of the harvest. Excessively humid conditions produce inferior crops, whereas dry weather often results in harvests of superior quality.

Higher **altitudes** also improve quality, but at the expense of output. In tropical regions, tea plants can be cultivated as high as 8,200 feet/2,500 m above sea level.

Sunlight is also an important factor, required for the formation of the essential oils that gives tea its aromas. Diffused light is the most beneficial, so tall trees are planted in regular rows on most plantations. They help to stabilize the ecology of the soil, as well as filtering the sunlight. Tea plants have a low tolerance for windy conditions and grow best in calm, pure air.

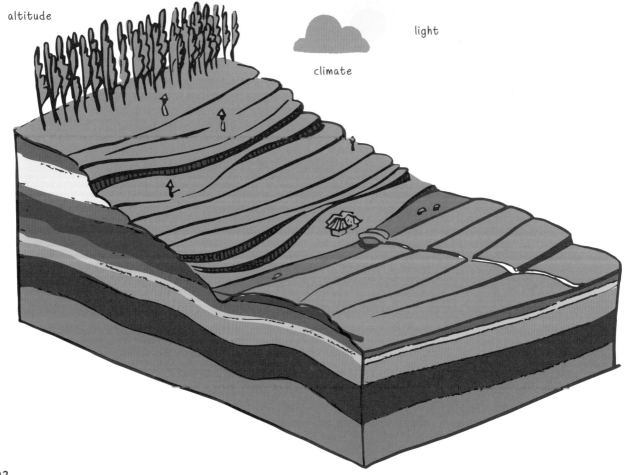

altitude

climate

light

CULTIVATION OF TEA PLANTS

Although tea was once grown from seeds, it is now generally propagated by taking cuttings from mature plants.

FROM CUTTING TO HARVEST

Cuttings are taken from the selected plants and transported to nurseries, where they remain for twelve to eighteen months. When they have matured into young plants, they are transferred back to the main plantation and replanted so that the shrubs cover the entire ground surface. The plant is allowed to mature for four years. Its height is maintained at about 4 feet/1.2 m to facilitate harvesting and provide the plant with a sturdy structure. Tea plants reach maturity at the end of the fifth year, when they begin normal production.

The plants are pruned from time to time to keep them at a height that facilitates plucking. A tea plant typically remains productive for no more than forty to fifty years. However, some varieties live as long as one hundred years. Harvesting commences at the end of the fifth year of cultivation. The leaves are plucked on seven- to fifteen-day cycles, depending on their growth rate, the weather conditions, and the quantity of tea to be harvested. Since tea is an evergreen plant, harvesting occurs throughout the year, except in plantations at very high altitudes.

TEA-PRODUCING COUNTRIES

- Tea-producing countries
- Tea-growing regions

MANUAL AND MECHANICAL HARVESTING

Manual harvesting is the most commonly practiced method, particularly for high-quality teas, which require the delicate touch that only a practiced hand can provide. In addition, many of the world's plantations are sited on precipitous slopes that are inaccessible to machines.

BY HAND

Harvesting is done by hand in China and Taiwan, where the tea gardens are small, often family-run, businesses. Manual picking is also widespread in India, and is used somewhat less frequently in Japan for the finest Gyokuro teas. Harvesting these plants requires dexterity and careful observation.

The pickers always face toward the slope, with both hands moving across the harvesting surface. The young sprig that is to be plucked is gripped between index and the middle fingers of each hand, broken off with the thumb, and grasped in the palm before being thrown backward over the shoulder into the sack or bag hung on the plucker's back. In one day, a worker can harvest up to 132 pounds/60 kg of leaves, which yield about 26.5 pounds/12 kg of tea when dried.

BY MACHINE

Mechanical harvesting is practiced in **areas where the cost of labor is relatively high**; its only advantage is that it reduces the need for employees. Some machines are capable of plucking only the first leaves, producing a good harvested product, but there is always a certain amount of wastage. More often, this mechanized process harvests the plants blindly, shearing off all the young sprouts without adjusting for the maturity of the bud.

The most frequently used machine is an automatic mower, which functions only in flat areas. It straddles the rows of plants and harvests an area about 5 feet/1.5 m wide.

CALENDAR OF GRANDS CRUS HARVESTS

Unlike the seasonally harvested crops familiar in most Western countries, tea is a member of the evergreen family. Harvesting could theoretically occur year round in cycles ranging from four to fifteen days. However, the tea plant grows more rapidly during hot, humid seasons and more slowly when the weather is cool, so the frequency of the harvests varies based on the season and time of year. The schedule also varies depending on the quality of the tea desired.

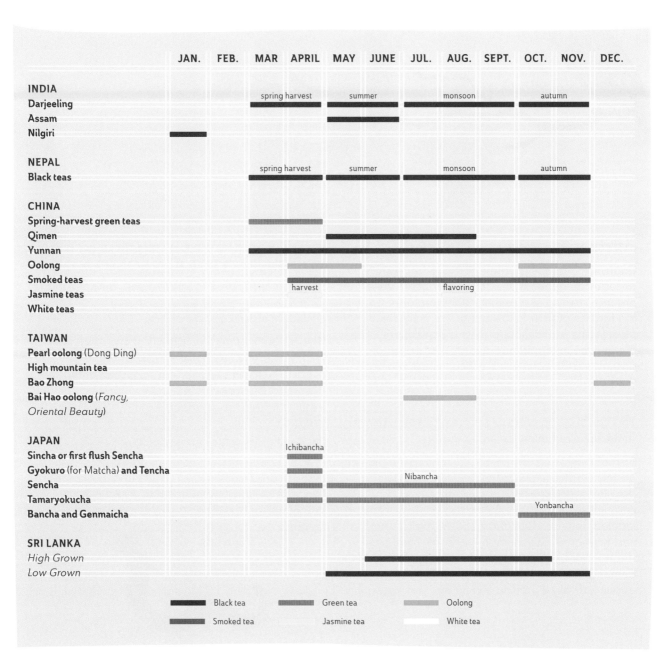

ORGANIC AGRICULTURE

Over the last twenty years, an increasing number of producers have adopted certified organic agricultural methods. Aware of the ecological concerns of their Western clients, many planters have realized the advantages of an environmentally sensitive approach.

ORGANIC CERTIFICATION

Confronted by the problem of soil exhaustion after decades of monoculture, some producers view organic farming as **a realistic solution** for restoring the fertility of their fields and preventing their plantations from falling prey to a slow but inexorable decline in output and quality. Others regard organic certification as an **official endorsement** that formally recognizes the clean agricultural practices that they have always followed.

This certification process represents a **significant financial investment** for a plantation.

At the conclusion of a so-called conversion period, during which the plantation must comply with a detailed set of specifications, it obtains a certificate allowing it to export its tea to Europe labeled as a "product of organic farming." This certification must accompany the merchandise throughout its shipment process and may be demanded at any time by the certifying entity, public authorities, or the consumer.

COMPOST, VERMICULTURE, AND OTHER "NATURAL" SOLUTIONS

The primary source of fertilizers is **compost**, made from the vegetable waste and manure that are available locally.

The practice of vermiculture is also becoming increasingly widespread. **Earthworms**, which are natural fertilizing agents, are introduced into the plantations. They enrich the soil with their castings, which contain an abundance of nutritional mineral elements.

There is also an organic solution to combating harmful parasites. Some growers are introducing **natural predators**, such as birds and insects that have been carefully selected to avoid introducing a species that could disrupt the ecosystem's balance.

FAIR TRADE TEA

Reflecting the concerns of Western consumers in the mid-1990s, fair trade advocates initially targeted the cocoa and coffee sectors. Tea is also subject to oversight by concerned tea dealers and consumers.

―――――

CERTIFICATION OF "FAIR TRADE" TEA

"Fair trade" certification is less common in the domain of tea than in coffee or cocoa, but this is not indicative of a lack of responsibility in the tea-growing world. Forced labor does not exist on tea plantations, and their working conditions do not impose the hardships that are prevalent for coffee or cocoa laborers. Needless to say, however, tea plantations' standards vary widely from country to country.

CHINA

China not only boasts the world's broadest and richest array of teas (there are thousands).
It also has a reputation for excellence, offering grands crus of the highest quality to impress and delight
the most demanding tea lovers.

CONSUMPTION

Although **China produces tea of every color** (see page 81), **green is the favorite for local consumption**. China consumes two thirds of what it produces: almost 75 percent of that is green, 20 percent is black and dark, and 5 percent is oolong. Other white and yellow teas are produced in very limited quantities. Per capita consumption of 13 ounces/370 g may seem low at first glance, but tea drinking plays an essential role in daily life. The Chinese prepare tea in a very distinctive fashion, reinfusing the same leaves all day long. Every morning, hundreds of millions of Chinese toss a handful of tea leaves into thermoses that are kept by their side throughout the day and refreshed regularly with additional boiling water.

Consumption of oolong and Pu Erh teas was for a long time limited to southern cities, such as Guangzhou or the Chinese communities in Hong Kong and abroad. In the last thirty years, tea houses have reopened; the rise of the upper middle class in the more prosperous coastal provinces has created a larger audience with renewed interest in quality tea. Prices have been subject to considerable inflationary pressure.

PRINCIPAL TEA-GROWING REGIONS

Tea cultivation is concentrated in the southeastern provinces, particularly Fujian, Zhejiang, Yunnan, Sichuan, Hunan, Hubei, and Anhui. Tea is grown in more than twenty Chinese provinces, which offer a wide range of contrasting climatic and geologic features. In some areas, tea is picked year-round, whereas harvests are seasonal elsewhere.

The regions producing the highest-quality teas are usually those that have mountainous landscapes of moderate altitude—from 1,640 to 3,940 feet/500 to 1,200 m—although in Yunnan, some plateaus are above 6,560 feet/2,000 m. Often, the name of the mountain is celebrated and associated with the tea produced on its slopes. It is somewhat similar to the French appellation system for wine; many Chinese villages with a distinctive expertise give their name to the teas they grow.

Fujian

＊ Most productive region (about 20 percent of China's total production)

＊ Largest variety of teas

＊ Birthplace of all processing methods (except those used for green and yellow teas)

＊ Three areas are particularly renowned: the environs of the city of Fuding, which produce the best white, green, and jasmine teas; the Wu Yi Shan mountain range that separates Fujian from Jiangxi, which is legendary for its oolong "cliff teas" and its smoked teas; and the Anxi district, which produces the best Tie Guan Yin teas.

Zhejiang

＊ The second most productive region (about 17 percent of China's total production)

＊ Green teas exclusively, of all qualities

＊ Gunpowder tea is produced on a massive industrial scale, often mediocre and intended solely for export. It originated in Zhejiang, as did Long Jing, an extraordinary artisanal green tea beloved by the Chinese.

Yunnan

＊ Yunnan has been one of the two largest producers of Chinese black tea for sixty years.

＊ The first tea plants almost certainly were grown in the forests of this province. Yunnan was the departure point for the first tea and horse trading routes. It still produces—and recently in spectacular quantities—the cakes of compressed tea that were first transported westward 1,500 years ago.

＊ The autonomous prefecture of Xishuangbanna and the district of Lincang, on the banks of the Mekong River, are the two principal regions producing the teas named after Pu Erh, the town through which the compressed tea trade route passed.

Anhui

＊ Limited production (about 6 percent of China's total production), but high quality

＊ This province is famed for its Huangshan mountain range, the birthplace of many of the best spring harvest green teas, as well as Qimen, a black tea whose reputation is legendary worldwide.

CHINA

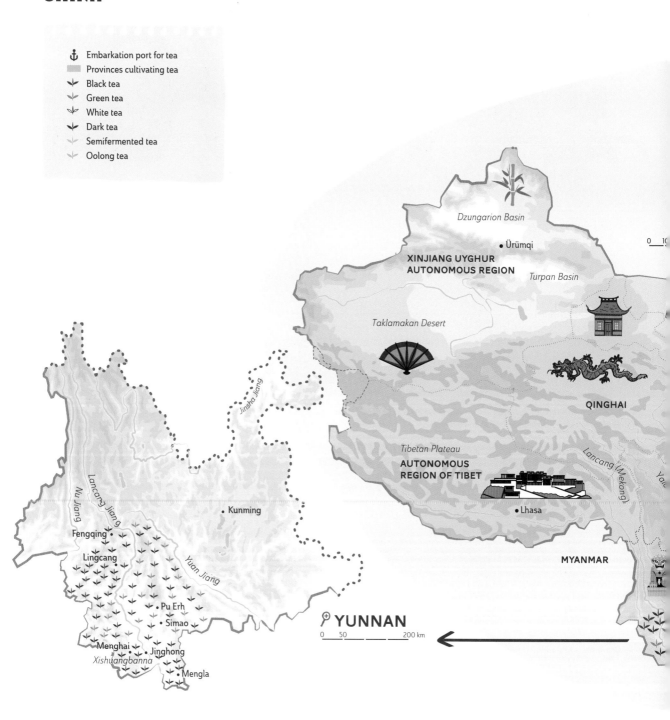

- ⚓ Embarkation port for tea
- ▨ Provinces cultivating tea
- 🌿 Black tea
- 🌿 Green tea
- 🌿 White tea
- 🌿 Dark tea
- 🌿 Semifermented tea
- 🌿 Oolong tea

Dzungarion Basin

• Ürümqi

0   10

**XINJIANG UYGHUR
AUTONOMOUS REGION**

Turpan Basin

Taklamakan Desert

Jinsha Jiang

QINGHAI

Tibetan Plateau

**AUTONOMOUS
REGION OF TIBET**

Lancang (Mekong)

Yal

• Lhasa

Kunming •

Nu Jiang

Lancang Jiang

MYANMAR

Fengqing •

Lingcang •

Yuan Jiang

• Pu Erh

• Simao

Menghai • • Jinghong

Xishuangbanna

• Mengla

⊕ **YUNNAN**

0   50   200 km

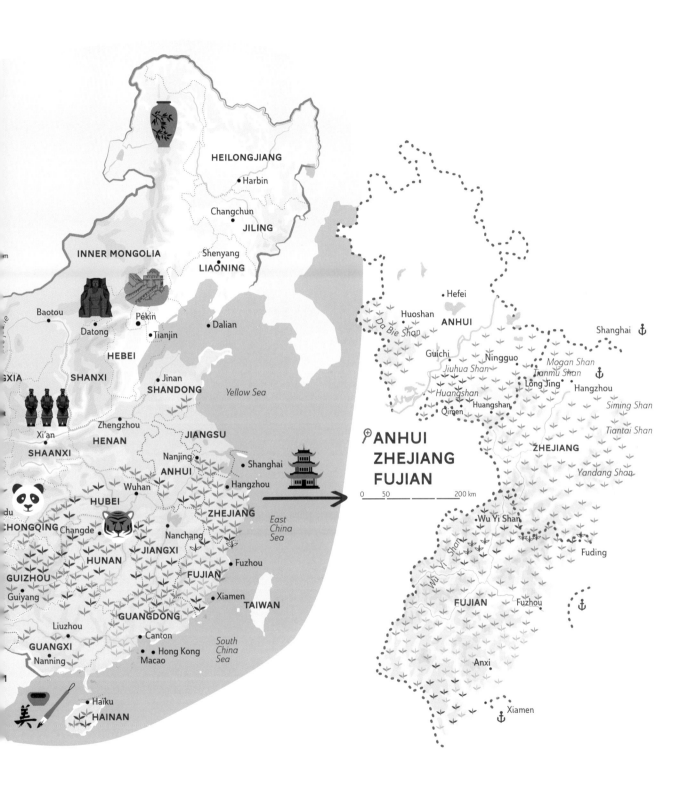

HEILONGJIANG

• Harbin

• Changchun
JILING

INNER MONGOLIA

• Shenyang
LIAONING

Baotou
Datong
Pékin
• Dalian
• Tianjin

HEBEI

SHANXI
GXIA
• Jinan
SHANDONG   *Yellow Sea*

Zhengzhou
• Zhengzhou   JIANGSU
Xi'an   Nanjing
HENAN   ANHUI   • Shanghai
SHAANXI   Wuhan   Hangzhou
                  HUBEI
CHONGQING Changde   ZHEJIANG
                              Nanchang   *East China Sea*
                  JIANGXI
HUNAN
GUIZHOU   FUZHOU Fuzhou
Guiyang   FUJIAN
                  • Xiamen
                              TAIWAN
          GUANGDONG
Liuzhou   • Canton
GUANGXI   • Hong Kong   *South China Sea*
Nanning   Macao

美
• Haïku
HAINAN

**ANHUI
ZHEJIANG
FUJIAN**

• Hefei

Huoshan   ANHUI
Da Bie Shan
Guichi   Ningguo   *Mogan Shan*   Shanghai ⚓
             Jiuhua Shan   *Tianmu Shan*
Huangshan   Long Jing Hangzhou
Qimen   Huangshan   *Siming Shan*
                                    Tiantai Shan
                         ZHEJIANG
                                Yandang Shan

• Wu Yi Shan

Wu Yi Shan
                                    • Fuding

FUJIAN   Fuzhou ⚓

0   50   200 km

• Anxi
⚓ Xiamen

TAIWAN

Taiwan now consumes most of its own production, consisting primarily of what
the Chinese call "blue-green" teas. The Taiwanese also drink green and jasmine teas, particularly
in restaurants. The immense success of Pu Erhs worldwide has also attracted the interest
of the local population in the last decade. The popularity of these dark teas now extends well beyond
the original tight-knit circle of enlightened connoisseurs.

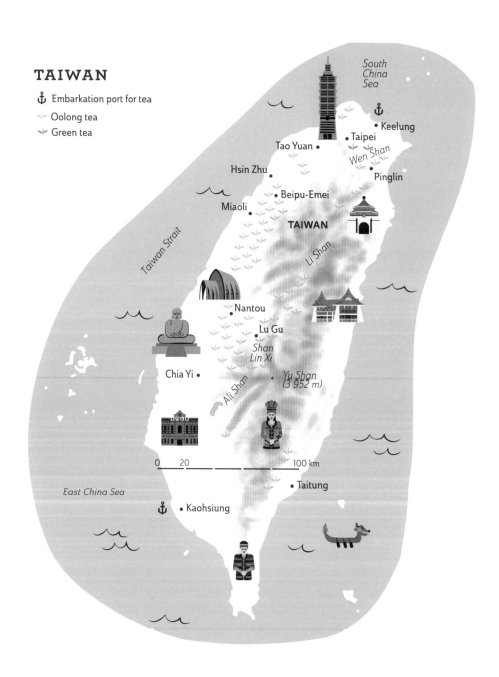

TAIWAN

⚓ Embarkation port for tea

🌿 Oolong tea

🌿 Green tea

South China Sea

• Keelung

• Taipei

Tao Yuan •

Wen Shan

Hsin Zhu

• Pinglin

• Beipu-Emei

Miaoli

TAIWAN

Taiwan Strait

Li Shan

• Nantou

Lu Gu

Shan Lin Xi

Chia Yi •

Yu Shan (3 952 m)

Ali Shan

0   20   100 km

East China Sea

• Taitung

⚓ • Kaohsiung

Since 1991, the island has been a net importer of tea, and the vast majority of these imports come from mainland China.

As in China, tea is an integral part of Taiwanese daily life. There is always a table especially dedicated to tea in homes and workplaces, a favored spot for conversation and debate. Tea is prepared following the rules of Gong Fu Cha, but in Taiwan, "teatime" is more elaborately observed than on the mainland, taking on ritual aspects.

Teahouses often offer teas of the highest quality, and they also host numerous activities and debates that further enhance the pleasures of tasting. These establishments are places of contrast, both havens of serenity remote from the outside world, and centers of cultural, intellectual, artistic, commercial, and often political life.

PRINCIPAL TEA-GROWING REGIONS

Located beneath the Tropic of Cancer, the island provides the ideal conditions for cultivating tea. Over half the territory has an altitude exceeding 650 feet/200 m, and numerous mountain ranges offer cool, moist conditions that are highly conducive to the production of fine-quality teas. Taiwan's best-known varieties are its "blue-green" (semioxidized) teas, which are divided into three categories: Bao Zhong, lightly oxidized; oolongs, rolled into pearls (Dong Ding, Jin Xuan, Gao Shan Cha, etc.); and Bai Hao oolongs.

Nantou District

✳ Leading tea-producing region overall on the island (about 50 percent of Taiwan's total production)

✳ The village of Lu Gu and its lake, the Taiwanese birthplace of Dong Ding teas, are between 1,640 and 2,620 feet/500 and 800 m in altitude. The Shan Lin Xi mountain range in the district's southeast, which rises to 5,900 feet/1,800 m high, produces some high-mountain teas (Gao Shan Cha). Nantou and its region produce primarily oolongs rolled into very dense pearls that the Taiwanese commonly refer to by the single term Wu Long, which can lead to confusion.

Taipei District

✳ The island's leading green tea–producing region

✳ Generally basic quality, with the exception of Pinglin, a village to the southeast of the capital, where Bao Zhong (lightly oxidized tea) has been produced for over a hundred years

Hsin Zhu District

✳ Birthplace of teas oxidized 60 percent or more

✳ A specialty that is genuinely unique in Taiwan, the finest specimens of Bai Hao oolong teas are often referred to as "Oriental Beauty." The best gardens are located in the villages of Beipu and Emei.

Chia Yi District

✳ About 10 percent of the island's total production

✳ This district, with its Alishan mountain range, is one of Taiwan's most highly regarded regions for high-mountain teas.

The plantations are between 3,280 and 4,920 feet/1,000 and 1,500 m above sea level.

Other Districts

✳ Significant amounts of tea are also grown in the districts of Taitung, Tao Yuan, and Miaoli.

JAPAN

Tea in all its forms is central to Japanese society, whether the daily brew served in restaurants (Bancha, Hojicha); the convivial, refined beverage tasted with small groups of friends (Gyokuro, Sencha); or the central aspect of the Zen aesthetic and philosophy expressed in Cha No Yu, the Japanese tea ceremony.

Tea is so thoroughly integrated into Japanese culture that there is a specific term (*o cha*) that designates Japanese tea (which is always green). It contrasts with *ko cha*, referring to all non-Japanese teas, often black varieties, oolongs, and flavored teas. Japan is a major importer of high-end Darjeelings and fine Chinese and Taiwanese exports.

It is the only country that consumes virtually the entirety of its production, which is actually not sufficient to meet internal demand. The Japanese have invested in China, Indonesia, and Vietnam, where they produce Sencha-type teas according to methods that are identical to those practiced in Japan itself. These are sold within the Japanese archipelago, and it is not always specified that they are imported.

PRINCIPAL TEA-GROWING REGIONS

The plantations are located in flat areas or hillsides in the southern part of the island nation, mostly in Honshu and Kyushu, between the 31st and 36th parallels. The climate there is relatively cool. temperatures and rainfall are fairly consistent throughout the entire archipelago. Production is almost exclusively confined to green tea processed by roasting. Despite the fifty-five official cultivars, the region is largely monocultural, growing mostly Yabukita teas. There are four harvests a year, and the first is by far the most prized.

Shizuoka Prefecture

✳ The plantations of Shizuoka are the southernmost tea-growing areas, along with Turkey and Georgia. Climatic conditions are challenging during much of the year, and this weather is key to the distinctive characteristics of Shizuoka teas.

✳ Sencha is the iconic tea of Shizuoka, which fabricates not only the tea leaves of its own plantations, but also those of the Honshu and Kyushu.

✳ There are two distinct steps in the Japanese method of processing tea, and these may occur at different times and places. The first is the production of raw tea, or Aracha; the second step refines the leaves and gives them their final form. Shizuoka has 81 square miles/21,000 hectares of gardens producing 45 percent of Japanese tea, and its factories process 70 percent of all the tea grown in Japan.

Kyoto Prefecture

✳ Although this area is less significant in terms of scale and production (slightly over 3 percent of total Japanese output), it is the birthplace of Japanese culture and the most prestigious appellation for Matcha, Gyokuro, and Sencha teas. The plantations are located around the town of Uji, southwest of Kyoto.

Kyushu Prefectures

✳ Kagoshima, Japan's second-largest tea-growing region, supplies 22 percent of the nation's output in terms of all types of tea combined. The other prefectures of Kyushu are the preferred locations for the production of Tamaryokucha.

JAPAN

Tea-producing prefectures

Green tea

0 5 ___ ___ 200 km

Hokkaido

Honshu

Sea of Japan

Sea of Japan

Maizuru

Fukuchiyama   Ayabe   Miyama

Kyoto

Uji

Joyo

IBARAKI

SAITAMA

GIFU

Tokyo

0 5 ___ ___ 20 km

KYOTO

KYOTO

AICHI   SHIZUOKA

Kyushu

NARA   MIE

SHIZUOKA

0 5 ___ ___ 20 km

Shikoku

FUKUOKA

SAGA   KOUCHI

NAGASAKI

KUMAMOTO

Mount Fuji
(3 776 m)

Fuji

MIYAZAKI

KAGOSHIMA

Shizuoka

Hamamatsu

INDIA

First introduced as an export crop by the British colonists, tea is now the national beverage of India. Domestic consumption, which was nil in 1850, now absorbs almost 80 percent of the country's output. Although green tea production was introduced in the 1990s, India produces black tea almost exclusively.

Tea is immensely popular in India in all strata of society. A few may cling to a traditionally British ritual of tea drinking, but the vast majority of Indians enjoy a daily treat known as chai, a delectable blend of black tea, spices, and sugar infused in boiling hot whole milk (see page 97). However, the very best Indian teas (particularly Darjeelings and the finest harvests of Assam), are far too costly for the local population and are exported.

PRINCIPAL TEA-GROWING REGIONS

The three principal tea-producing regions are Darjeeling, Assam, and Nilgiri. There are other areas that are less significant in terms of both quality and quantity.

Darjeeling

✳ The region of Darjeeling (only slightly over 1 percent of India's output) is the country's best-known and most prestigious appellation.

✳ There are eighty-seven tea gardens under cultivation, located 1,310 to 8,200 feet/400 to 2,500 m above sea level. The region produces almost exclusively traditional black tea, along with a very small amount of oolong and green teas. The quality of the crops varies widely, and the price differential between standard and truly great grands crus can vary by 100 percent.

✳ Given their extremely high prices, Darjeelings are almost entirely reserved for export. Their reputation is so elevated that Darjeelings are subject to a rate of counterfeiting unmatched elsewhere in the world of tea.

✳ Each of the four annual harvests has a distinctive taste profile. Springtime and summer harvests are the most prized. The July–August monsoon crop is of mediocre quality.

Assam

✳ Assam is located in northeastern India between Bangladesh, Myanmar, and China. It is a low-lying, very fertile region, traversed by the Brahmaputra River and its tributaries. The land was a tropical forest until the nineteenth century, but it now produces almost half of all Indian tea. Four harvests are possible (spring, summer, monsoon, and autumn), but the springtime crop is only rarely plucked; it is much less sought after than the summer harvest. Most production occurs between April and October. In addition to the very large plantations of greater than 1,235 acres/500 hectares, about 40,000 independent farms grow their own leaves and sell them in bulk to manufacturers.

Nilgiri

✳ Nilgiri, located in southern India, is the second-largest tea-producing area. In contrast to Darjeeling and Assam, tea is harvested year-round without interruption. Almost the entire region makes CTC black teas (see page 89). Teas grown here are undistinguished, and good plantations can be numbered on the fingers of one hand.

Kangra

✳ The British began growing tea in this region close to Kashmir in the nineteenth century. Several of these gardens have begun to produce very good teas in recent years.

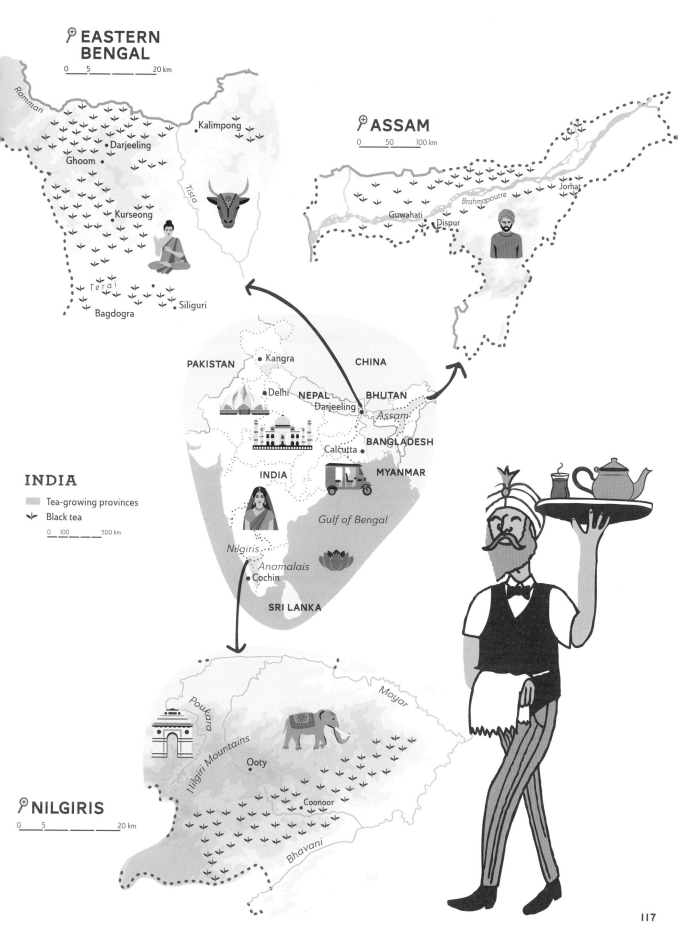

0   5   20 km

Ramman

Kalimpong

Darjeeling

Ghoom

Tista

Kurseong

T e r a i

Siliguri

Bagdogra

⚲ ASSAM

0   50   100 km

Brahmapoutre

Jorhat

Guwahati

Dispur

PAKISTAN   Kangra   CHINA

Delhi   NEPAL   BHUTAN

Darjeeling   *Assam*

BANGLADESH

Calcutta

INDIA   MYANMAR

INDIA

▨ Tea-growing provinces

↯ Black tea

0   100   500 km

Nilgiris

Anamalais
Cochin

Gulf of Bengal

SRI LANKA

Poukara

Moyar

Nilgiri Mountains

Ooty

Coonoor

⚲ NILGIRIS

0   5   20 km

Bhavani

NEPAL

Nepal produces mostly black teas, primarily for the tea bag market. However, grands crus represent about a sixth of its output.

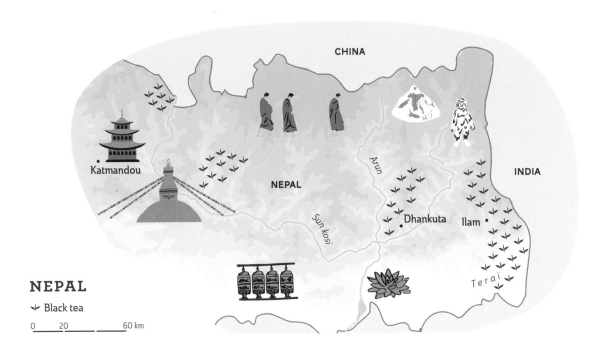

NEPAL

⤸ Black tea

0   20   60 km

High-quality black teas are produced primarily in Ilam and Dhankuta. They are routinely exported, often at very high prices. In the far eastern part of the country near the city of Ilam, it is not uncommon for newly harvested leaves to be fraudulently transported to India rather than being processed locally. There are Darjeeling plantation owners on the other side of the border who have no scruples about buying tea from Nepal to add to their own harvest and increase their production.

PRINCIPAL TEA-GROWING REGIONS

There are three tea-producing regions in Nepal.

✱ The teas of **Terai** are lowland teas that have little to recommend them and are primarily used for CTC production (see page 89).

✱ **Ilam** produces some decent teas, but too often seeks to mimic Darjeelings.

✱ **Dhankuta** is a more interesting case. Its plantations go back only fifteen to twenty years, and were planted with young tea plants selected from the best varieties. Tea grows at between 3,930 and 7,210 feet/1,200 and 2,200 m above sea level in this region. The harvest schedule in Ilam and Dhankuta is exactly the same as that of Darjeeling. Small producers play an important role here because there are no large-scale plantations on the British model. In these mountainous landscapes, tea is cultivated according to "clean" agricultural practices that protect wooded areas.

SRI LANKA

Sri Lanka produces black tea almost exclusively, and it is generally cultivated using traditional methods. CTC (see page 89) was introduced in the early 1990s, but it represents no more than 10 percent of the total production. Most of the output is processed by machine (using Rotorvane equipment that chops and crushes the leaves).

Sri Lanka, one of the largest tea producers, exports almost 95 percent of its tea. While tea plants are ubiquitous in the island landscape, tea has oddly little visibility in Sri Lankan culture. Annual per capita consumption of 2.2 pounds/1.2 kg is certainly evidence of widespread habitual use, but in contrast to most other tea-growing nations, there are no particular traditions attached to the beverage.

PRINCIPAL TEA-GROWING REGIONS

Despite its relatively small area, Sri Lanka boasts contrasting climatic zones with monsoons occurring twice a year. Varying sharply from one tea-growing region to another, the seasons are very different and harvest schedules are unpredictable. Tea is grown in six principal areas: **Galle, Ratnapura, Kandy, Nuwara Eliya, Dimbula**, and **Uva**.

The island's teas are customarily distinguished by the altitude (up to 7,210 feet/2,200 m above sea level) **at which they are cultivated, rather than the location where they grow.**

Teas grown below 1,970 feet/600 m are called "low grown"; from 1,970 to 3,930 feet/600 to 1,200 m, mid grown; and above 3,930 feet/ 1,200 m, high grown. The latter are considered superior, a point of view not always shared in the rest of the tea drinking world.

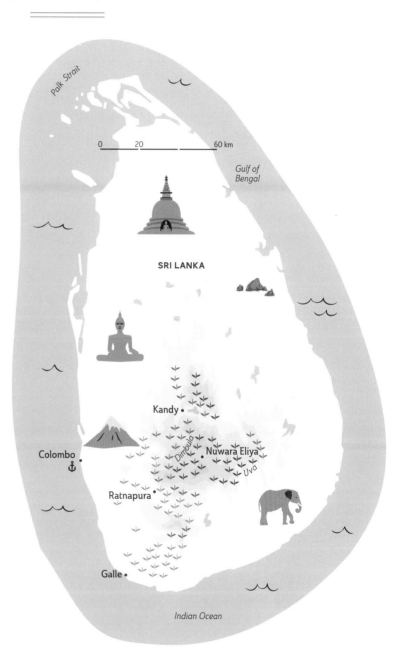

SRI LANKA

⚓ Embarkation port for tea

Black teas
- ↘ *low grown* (less than 1,970 feet/600 m above sea level)
- ↘ *mid-grown* (from 1,970 to 3,930 feet/600 to 1,200 m above sea level)
- ↘ *high grown* (more than 3,930 feet/1,200 m above sea level)

SOUTH KOREA

*Despite its ancient history, Korea is not a major tea producer
nor an avid consumer. Nevertheless, tea occupies an important place in the
Korean national consciousness. People are very attached to this aspect of their patrimony,
which they have reclaimed since the end of the Second World War.*

Most teas produced in Korea are sold domestically. They are considered very prestigious and are usually quite expensive. Tea is often presented as a gift and served on important occasions, frequently as part of an elaborate ceremony.

With the exception of Jukro, Korea produces exclusively green teas, harvested in spring and processed in a variety of ways.

Jeoncha is a roasted green tea very similar to Japanese Sencha, harvested and processed in early April. Woojeon, known for its lovely twisted leaves, is produced at the same time of year. Sejak is harvested later in mid-May, and is a less delicate type that includes a bud and two leaves.

PRINCIPAL TEA-GROWING REGIONS

There are three tea-producing areas, all located on the southern part of the country.

✳ The historic region is **the province of South Gyeongsang**, particularly around the village of Hadong. Korea's oldest tea plantations are in this area, located on the slopes of the Jirisan Mountains.

✳ A bit farther west, **the district of Boseong**, in the province of South Jeolla, is the peninsula's other large cultivation zone.

✳ Finally, the most magnificent plantations are found on **the island of Jeju**. This beautifully preserved volcanic island combines all the conditions most favorable for tea cultivation: ideal soils, a mild, humid climate, and ample sunshine and rainfall.

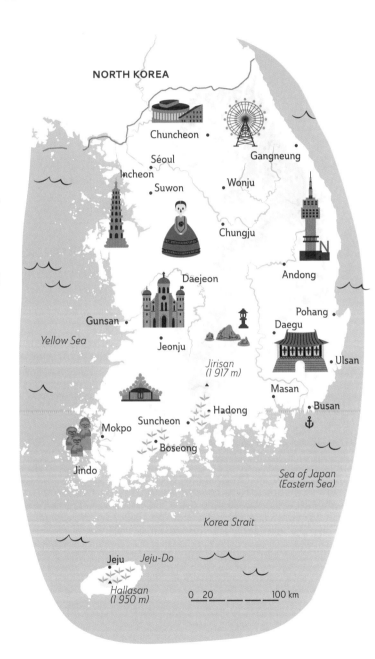

SOUTH KOREA

⤹ Green tea

⚓ Embarkation point for tea

OTHER TEA-PRODUCING COUNTRIES IN ASIA

About a dozen other Asian nations cultivate tea. Some, including Thailand and Laos,
have developed tea-growing cultures under the tutelage of China. Others,
such as Malaysia, Indonesia, and Bangladesh, have colonial or postcolonial influences.
The socioeconomic organization and types of teas these countries produce reflect their histories.

THAILAND

Tea cultivation was introduced in the 1980s by the Chinese community that settled in the Mae Salong region in northern Thailand. Based on cultivars and techniques that originated in Taiwan, semi-oxidized teas of excellent quality are produced in small quantities.

LAOS

Small-scale coffee producers in southern Laos, hard hit by falling prices, began growing tea plants among their coffee crops to provide supplementary income. Tea cultivation in the country's north near the Chinese border has been practiced for centuries; here, they produce primarily compressed teas from wild plants.

MYANMAR

This country, the historic birthplace of tea, lies between Laos and China. Tea grows wild in the forests, and the Burmese have harvested and produced tea throughout their history.

Tea cultivation has also developed in the country's mountainous north and east, strongly influenced by the manufacturing practices of the neighboring Chinese province of Yunnan.

AND ALSO...

Vietnam
Malaysia
Indonesia
Bangladesh
Papua New Guinea

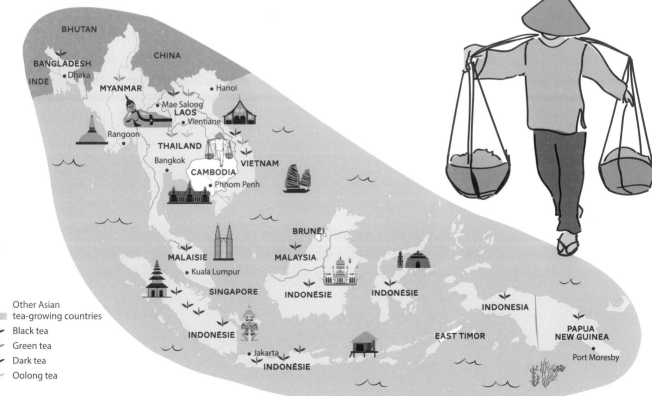

Other Asian tea-growing countries
Black tea
Green tea
Dark tea
Oolong tea

AFRICA

Tea was first introduced to Africa in the late nineteenth century, beginning in Malawi and South Africa, where the British encouraged its cultivation to provide additional sources of supply. Subsequently, German colonists began growing tea on the slopes of Mount Cameroon and in Tanzania. Many other African countries also adopted tea cultivation during the twentieth century, and the continent is now one of the leading players in the international tea trade

PRINCIPAL TEA-PRODUCING COUNTRIES

Kenya
Malawi
Uganda
Burundi
Tanzania
Mozambique
Rwanda
Zimbabwe
Ethiopia
Cameroon
Congo
Mauritius
South Africa
Zambia
Reunion
Madagascar
Mali
Seychelles

Africa's teas are primarily classified as CTC (see page 89). But alongside this mass production, artisanal growers are experimenting with teas inspired by recent developments in China, India, and Japan. Following the example of other tea-growing regions, such as Nepal, some plantation managers have recently improved their quality, and grand cru teas are beginning to appear in Rwanda, Kenya, and Burundi.

AFRICA

- Tea-growing countries
- ↘ Black tea

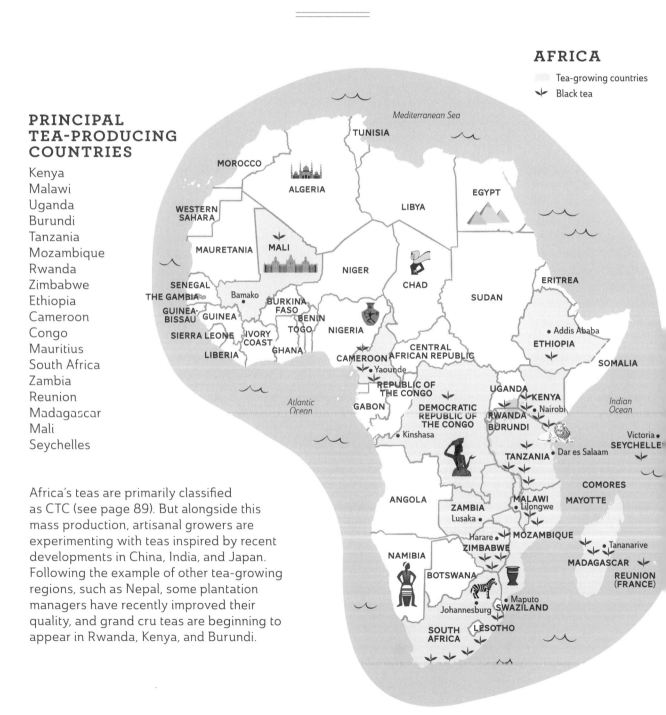

AROUND THE BLACK AND CASPIAN SEAS

Tea was introduced to this region via various trade routes, and was initially a luxury commodity imported from distant locations. It wasn't until much later that tea became a part of the indigenous culture.

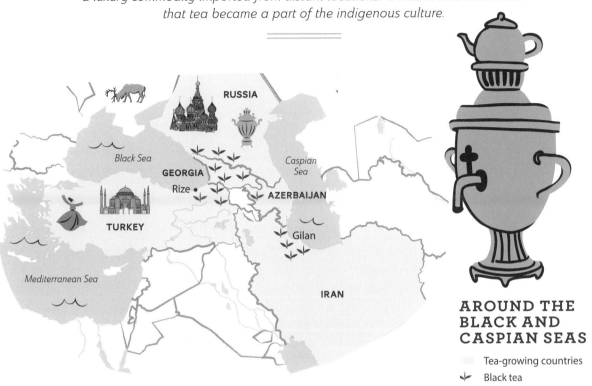

AROUND THE BLACK AND CASPIAN SEAS

- Tea-growing countries
- Black tea

The Mongols and the merchants who traveled the Silk Road are credited with bringing tea to the inhabitants of Russia, Turkey, Persia, and Kyrgyzstan, as well as to the Turkmens and Uzbeks. It was not until the late nineteenth and early twentieth centuries that tea cultivation became established after numerous failed attempts. Tea finally began to be successfully grown in the mountainous areas between the Black and Caspian Seas.

RUSSIAN TEAS

Specializing in black teas prepared in a samovar, Iran, Turkey, and Russia produce tea primarily for domestic consumption. With extensive plantations located in Georgia, the former USSR was once the world's fifth-largest tea producer. Teas from Russia are sometimes referred to as "Russian teas," because they are prepared in a samovar. They should not be confused with "Russian-style" varieties: these are blended Chinese black teas, sometimes flavored, that were fashionable in the Russian court at the end of the nineteenth century.

TURKEY

Tea consumption preceded tea cultivation in Turkey, as was the case for most other countries in this region. Tea was first introduced to the Ottoman court in the fifteenth century, but it was not cultivated until the 1920s, using seeds imported from the USSR. The plantations, mostly small, are located on the south coast of the Black Sea. Turkey is the world's sixth-largest tea producer; its output covers its own internal consumption and leaves a small amount for export.

Iran, Georgia, Azerbaijan, Montenegro, and **Russia** are also among the region's tea-producing countries.

SOUTH AMERICA

Completely unfamiliar to European consumers, South American teas make no pretense of competing with the great teas of Asia. Exclusively black teas with characteristics adapted to the "British taste," they are primarily produced for the tea bag and American soft drink markets.

ARGENTINA

Argentina is the only major tea producer in South America and the ninth largest in the world. However, most of us associate Argentina and its neighbor Brazil with the yerba maté plant, which is used to make the popular South American beverage, maté.

OTHER TEA-PRODUCING COUNTRIES

Peru
Ecuador
Bolivia
Brazil
Guatemala
El Salvador
Panama
Colombia

THERE'S TEA IN THOSE "PLANT EXTRACTS"...

The mysterious ingredient that appears on the labels of so many carbonated beverages is none other than tea, sometimes combined with guarana, a tropical plant whose seeds have a high caffeine content. So, inside every cola drinker lurks an unsuspecting tea tippler...

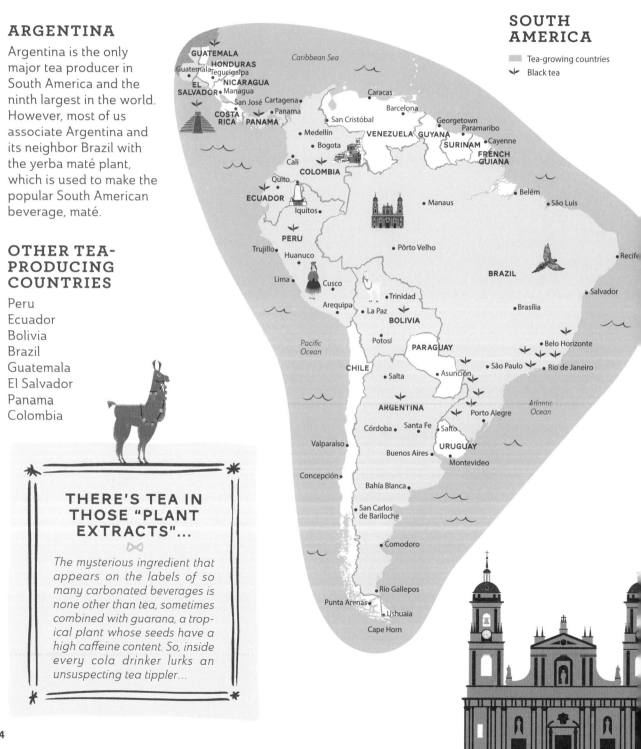

SOUTH AMERICA

Tea-growing countries
Black tea

SOCIAL AND ECONOMIC ASPECTS OF TEA

The world of tea presents an array of contrasting scenarios. These range from the few acres cultivated by a Nepalese farmer and his family, to the medium-size plantations that emerged following liberalization in China, to the vast plantations of Sri Lanka.

VARIOUS SYSTEMS OF ORGANIZATION

✱ The farmer grower

In many Asian countries, small units, often family operated, play a significant role in the tea economy. The farmer cultivates tea plants on his land and harvests his crop. Sometimes—as is often the case in China, Sri Lanka, and Nepal—his work stops there. He sells the fresh tea leaves in the local market, usually to another farmer operating on a larger scale with the facilities necessary for processing the leaves.

✱ Farmer-organized cooperatives

If the farmer has invested with his neighbors to form a cooperative, and has the equipment necessary to treat the leaves, he processes his own harvest, which he then sells to wholesalers. This is often the case in Japan, India, and Nepal.

✱ The farmer who harvests and processes his own tea

Sometimes, particularly in China and Taiwan, the farmer personally invests in his own equipment. He therefore sells fully processed tea to wholesalers and exporters, or sometimes deals directly with retailers.

✱ Companies that grow and manufacture tea

In India, Sri Lanka, and China, small family units coexist with vast entities that sometimes own plantations of hundreds, or even thousands, of acres/hectares, often employing thousands of laborers.

In the Indian subcontinent, very large plantations are frequently operated by major family groups or multinationals. In India, these businesses are never actually owners of the land; they have long-term leases from the government. These operators have a variety of obligations, including the duty to provide housing, health care, and education to their employees.

In the twentieth century, the Chinese government began to organize the production of teas that are not consumed locally and are intended for the export market (gunpowder, black teas, and smoked teas). Extremely large factories have been built for this purpose.

THE
FAMILIES
OF TEA

Look for Silver Needles, Yin Zen, Bai Mu Dan, and Bai Hao Yin Zen.

CHINESE WHITE TEA

China's white teas are produced from a cultivar known as Da Bai ("tall white"), an allusion to the impressive size of the plant's downy buds. Very subtle and thirst-quenching, white teas are rare and costly. They must be prepared with the utmost care to bring out their highly distinctive qualities.

WHITE TEA ✳ CHINA (FUJIAN) ✳ HARVESTED MARCH–EARLY APRIL

PREPARATION

With a tasting set: 5 to 10 minutes in 158°F/70°C water

In a Zhong: fill the Zhong halfway full with leaves (without tamping them down). Cover with water cooled to 158°F/70°C. Empty out this first infusion after just 10 seconds, and continue with additional brief infusions lasting less than a minute, gradually increasing the brewing times.

AROMATIC PROFILE

Profile: grassy/woodsy

Color of the liquor: straw

Astringency: subtle astringency when the infusion time is prolonged

Taste: very subtly sweet

DOMINANT AROMAS

vanilla · hay · miel honey · resinous wood · wicker

SECONDARY AROMAS

mint · rose · cocoa · thyme

SUGGESTED PAIRING

Delicious with fruit salad

Look for Tai Ping Hou Kui, Huangshan Mao Feng, Huang Hua Yun Jian, Long Jing, Bi Luo Chun, Bai Mao Hou, and hundreds of others!

CHINESE GREEN SPRING HARVEST TEA

Very sought after, these teas are harvested around April 5, when the Qing Ming festival is celebrated and the graves of ancestors are honored. The leaves of these Chinese green teas are available in many forms (folded, rolled, twisted, and shaped). Each village has its own traditions and specialties.

GREEN TEA ✳ CHINA (FUJIAN, ZHEJIANG, JIANGSU, ANHUI...) ✳ HARVESTED IN SPRING

PREPARATION

With a tasting set: 4 minutes in 167°F/75°C water

In a Zhong: repeated (up to 4 times), brief (30- to 40-second) infusions or a single, longer infusion (3 to 4 minutes), according to your preference.

AROMATIC PROFILE

Profile: grassy/fruity

Color of the liquor: pale gold

Astringency: subtle astringency

Taste: mild acidity and umami, sometimes a trace of bitterness

SUGGESTED PAIRING

Delicious with steamed fish

DOMINANT AROMAS

mango · artichoke · zucchini · chestnut · hazelnut

SECONDARY AROMAS

rose · flint · raw fish · licorice · mint

Look for Shincha and Sencha-Ichibancha with the name of the plantation or the grower.

JAPANESE GREEN SPRING HARVEST TEA

The year's first harvest ("Ichibancha" in Japanese) is eagerly anticipated throughout the island nation. Very tender and plucked at peak freshness, the young sprouts are made into "new teas" ("Shincha") that hold the promise of gustatory delights.

GREEN TEA ✳ JAPAN (SHIZUOKA, UJI, KAGOSHIMA...) ✳ HARVESTED IN APRIL

PREPARATION

With a tasting set: 2 minutes in 167°F/75°C water

In a Kyusu teapot: as described on page 66

AROMATIC PROFILE

Profile: grassy/iodine

Color of the liquor: pale green

Astringency: no astringency

Taste: mild bitterness. which is accentuated if prepared in a Kyusu

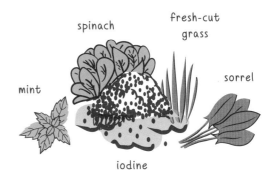

spinach

fresh-cut grass

sorrel

mint

iodine

DOMINANT AROMAS

SUGGESTED PAIRING

Delicious with a seafood platter

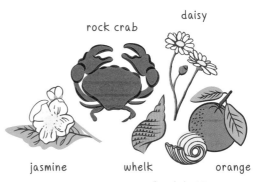

rock crab

daisy

jasmine

whelk

orange

fresh butter

SECONDARY AROMAS

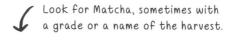

Look for Matcha, sometimes with a grade or a name of the harvest.

MATCHA

Matcha is the fabled tea used in the Japanese ceremony of Cha No Yu.
It is made from shade-grown "Tencha" leaves. Unlike the Gyokuro teas, whose leaves are shaped into needles, these are passed through a milling process until they are reduced to a beautiful jade-colored powder. This tea is frequently used as an ingredient in contemporary recipes.

GREEN TEA ✳ JAPAN (UJI, SHIZUOKA) ✳ HARVESTED IN APRIL

PREPARATION

With a whisk: as described on pages 64–65

AROMATIC PROFILE

Profile: grassy/iodine

Color of the liquor: deep green

Astringency: low astringency

Taste: bitter

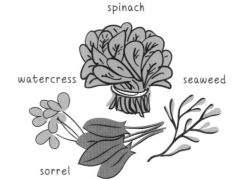

spinach

watercress

seaweed

sorrel

DOMINANT AROMAS

SUGGESTED PAIRING

Delicious with a marzipan dessert recipe

milk

cocoa

mint

vanilla

SECONDARY AROMAS

131

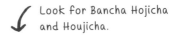

Look for Bancha Hojicha and Houjicha.

HOJICHA

In the 1920s, tea producers in Kyoto began roasting their green teas like coffee beans, at very high temperatures for several minutes. Extremely popular in Japan, this tea is almost invariably served in restaurants specializing in raw fish.

ROASTED GREEN TEA ✳ JAPAN (KAGOSHIMA) ✳ HARVESTED IN SEPTEMBER

PREPARATION

With a tasting set: 4 to 5 minutes in 203°F/95°C water

In a 10-ounce/300 ml teapot: 5 teaspoons/15 g of tea in 203°F/95°C water for 30 seconds

AROMATIC PROFILE

Profile: fruity/woodsy/toasted

Color of the liquor: mahogany

Astringency: no astringency

Taste: mildly sweet

pine
vanilla
blackberry
cedar

DOMINANT AROMAS

SUGGESTED PAIRING

Delicious with sushi and sashimi

grilled fish
apricot
cinnamon
plum
candied fruit

SECONDARY AROMAS

Look for Jeoncha, Woojeon, Sejak, and Jejudo.

SOUTH KOREAN GREEN TEA

Midway between Japanese green teas, with their creamy and grassy bouquet, and Chinese green teas, with their fruity mineral notes, Korean green teas are highly distinctive but little known outside the country.

GREEN TEA ✳ SOUTH KOREA (JEJU, HADONG) ✳ HARVESTED MAY–JUNE

PREPARATION

With a tasting set: 4 minutes in 75°C water

In a 10-ounce/300 m teapot: 4 to 5 teaspoons/8 to 10 g in 167°F/75°C water for 3 to 5 minutes

AROMATIC PROFILE

Profile: grassy/marine

Color of the liquor: bright green

Astringency: subtle astringency

Taste: umami with an acidic edge

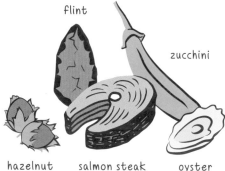

flint

zucchini

hazelnut   salmon steak   oyster

DOMINANT AROMAS

SUGGESTED PAIRING

Delicious with fresh pasta

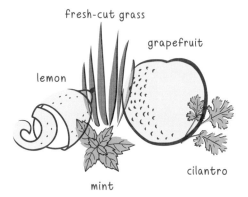

fresh-cut grass

grapefruit

lemon

mint

cilantro

SECONDARY AROMAS

Look for the name of the plantation if the
tea comes from a single known source. ↓

NEPALESE GREEN TEA

In the last fifteen years, Nepal has begun to produce excellent teas, first in the
Dhankuta region and subsequently in the Ilam valley. These teas, grown from young,
top-quality cultivars, are processed artisanally and vary widely in their processing methods.
(White, green, black, and oolong teas are all produced in Nepal.)

GREEN TEA ✳ NEPAL (ILAM AND DHANKUTA VALLEYS)
HARVESTED IN SPRING AND SUMMER

PREPARATION

With a tasting set: 3 to 4 minutes
in 80°C water

In a 10-ounce/300 ml teapot:
4 to 5 teaspoons/8 to 10 g in
176°F/80°C water for 3 to 4
minutes

AROMATIC PROFILE

Profile: grassy/mineral/fruity

Color of the liquor: pale yellow

Astringency: delicate astringency

Taste: a hint of acidity and
bitterness

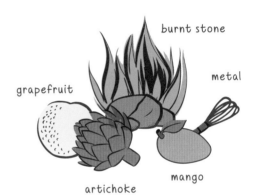

burnt stone

metal

grapefruit

mango

artichoke

DOMINANT
AROMAS

SUGGESTED PAIRING

Delicious with grilled fish

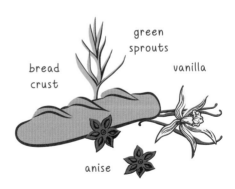

green
sprouts

bread
crust

vanilla

anise

SECONDARY
AROMAS

Look for Bao Zhong, Pouchong, Dong Ding,
Gao Shan Cha, and Jin Shuen.

LIGHTLY OXIDIZED TAIWANESE OOLONG

*These oolongs, oxidized from 10 to 40 percent, are icons of Taiwanese culture.
With the exception of Bao Zhong, whose leaves are simply crumpled, the teas are
rolled into large pearls that unfurl in the course of successive Gong Fu Cha infusions.
The very finest of these teas are grown in the mountain range in the center of the island
and are called Gao Shan Chaqui ("tea of the high mountain").*

**SEMIOXIDIZED TEA ✳ TAIWAN (DISTRICTS OF TAIPEI, NANTOU, AND CHIA YI)
HARVESTED IN SPRING AND WINTER**

PREPARATION

With a tasting set: 6 to 7 minutes
in 203°F/95°C water

Gong Fu Cha method: 4 to 6
successive infusions of 20 to 40
seconds

AROMATIC PROFILE

Profile: grassy/floral

Color of the liquor: golden yellow

Astringency: subtle astringency

Taste: slight acidity and sometimes
a hint of sweetness

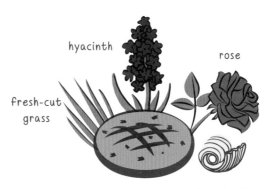

hyacinth

rose

fresh-cut
grass

marzipan   fresh butter

**DOMINANT
AROMAS**

SUGGESTED PAIRING

Delicious with all cream-based
desserts, such as crème brûlée or
egg custard

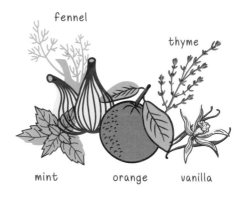

fennel

thyme

mint   orange   vanilla

**SECONDARY
AROMAS**

↳ Look for Anxi Tie Guan Yin, Huang Jing Gui, Ti Kwan Yin, and Tieh Kuan Yin.

LIGHTLY OXIDIZED CHINESE OOLONG

These teas have quite a long history, originating in the Qing Dynasty. They have become phenomenally popular in China over the last ten years. Very lightly oxidized (10 percent), they are processed from the leaves of two extraordinarily fragrant cultivars that produce intensely floral teas.

SEMIOXIDIZED ✹ CHINA (FUJIAN) ✹ HARVESTED IN SPRING AND AUTUMN

PREPARATION

In a tasting set: 6 to 7 minutes in 203°F/95°C water

Gong Fu Cha method: 4 to 6 successive infusions of 20 to 40 seconds

AROMATIC PROFILE

Profile: floral/milky

Color of the liquor: golden yellow

Astringency: no astringency

Taste: a hint of bitterness

SUGGESTED PAIRING

Delicious with fresh fruits

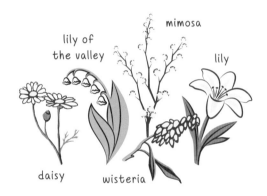

lily of the valley

mimosa

lily

daisy

wisteria

DOMINANT AROMAS

honey

condensed milk

vanilla

jasmine

fresh butter

SECONDARY AROMAS

Look for Bai Hao Oolong, Oriental Beauty, and Oolong Fancy.

DEEPLY OXIDIZED TAIWANESE TEA

These teas, which may be up to 70 percent oxidized, owe their unique fragrance to a natural occurrence: their leaves are attacked by an insect known as a leafhopper or a "green fly." The insect's damage inhibits the growth of the young sprouts and alters the chemical composition of the leaf. After oxidation, the antibodies produced by the plant create very distinctive flavor notes, both fruity and woodsy.

SEMIOXIDIZED ✳ TAIWAN (DISTRICT OF HSIN ZHU) ✳ HARVESTED IN SUMMER

PREPARATION

In a tasting set: 6 to 7 minutes in 203°F/95°C water

Gong Fu Cha method: 5 to 7 successive infusions of 20 to 40 seconds

AROMATIC PROFILE

Profile: woodsy/fruity

Color of the liquor: coppery

Astringency: no astringency

Taste: neutral

SUGGESTED PAIRING

Delicious with a tasting of grand cru chocolates

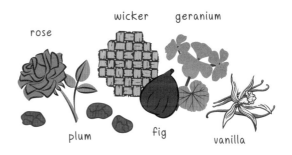

rose · wicker · geranium · plum · fig · vanilla

DOMINANT AROMAS

licorice · leather · apricot · cinnamon · raisin

SECONDARY AROMAS

Look for Feng Huang Dan Cong,
Phoenix Tea, Rou Gui, and Mi Lan Xian.

DAN CONG OOLONG

*These teas originated in the Feng Huang mountains of Guangdong,
The name ("Dan Cong" refers to "single plant") is a reminder that they are the product
of a tradition very remote from modern agricultural methods. Each tea plant
produces a unique tea. These ancient traditions are still observed for the most prestigious
varieties, which are harvested from the centuries-old plants.*

SEMIOXIDIZED TEA ✳ CHINA (GUANGDONG) ✳ HARVESTED IN APRIL–MAY

PREPARATION

With a tasting set: 6 to 7 minutes in 203°F/95°C water

Gong Fu Cha method: 5 to 7 successive infusions of 20 to 40 seconds

AROMATIC PROFILE

Profile: floral/fruity

Color of the liquor: coppery

Astringency: marked astringency

Taste: mildly bitter

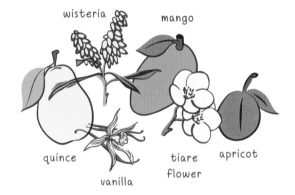

wisteria

mango

quince

vanilla

tiare flower

apricot

DOMINANT AROMAS

SUGGESTED PAIRING

Delicious with assorted tapas

green sprouts

sage

mint

orange

SECONDARY AROMAS

Look for Bohea, Ta Hong Pao, and Xia Hong Pao. ↘

DA HONG PAO

Grown in the northern reaches of the Wu Yi Sha Mountains in Fujian, Da Hong Pao ("big red robe") is one of China's legendary teas, named for the red color of its shrubs. There is also a "little red robe," Xiao Hong Pao, which is made from smaller leaves from the same tea plants.

SEMIOXIDIZED TEA ✳ CHINA (FUJIAN) ✳ HARVESTED MID-MAY

PREPARATION

With a tasting set: 6 to 7 minutes in 203°F/95°C water

Gong Fu Cha method: successive infusions of 30 to 60 seconds, as many times as you wish!

AROMATIC PROFILE

Profile: fruity/roasted

Color of the liquor: mahogany

Astringency: subtle astringency

Taste: neutral

roasted coffee · blackberry · plum · cinnamon · tobacco

DOMINANT AROMAS

SUGGESTED PAIRING

Delicious with madeleines

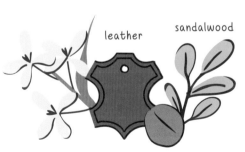

leather · sandalwood · osmanthus · dried apricot

SECONDARY AROMAS

Look for spring-harvest Darjeeling and Nepal, with or without the mention of the cultivar "AV2" or the name of the plantation, if the tea comes from a single known source.

HIMALAYAN "AV2"

The springtime harvest in Darjeeling and Nepal is largely determined by the weather conditions during the preceding months, as well as by the type of tea plant harvested. New plantations have been established in Nepal during the last few decades, and, with the reforestation of land planted by the British in the nineteenth century, new cultivars have been planted. One of these, known as AV2, produces teas of excellent quality.

**BLACK TEA ✳ INDIA (DARJEELING) AND NEPAL (DHANKUTA, ILAM)
HARVESTED IN MARCH–APRIL**

PREPARATION

With a tasting set: 3 minutes in 185°F/85°C water

In a 10-ounce/300 ml teapot: 4 to 5 teaspoons/8 to 10 g of tea in 185°F/85°C water for 3 minutes

AROMATIC PROFILE

Profile: floral/grassy/zesty

Color of the liquor: gold

Astringency: delicate astringency

Taste: slight acidity and mild bitterness

DOMINANT AROMAS

SUGGESTED PAIRING

Delicious with scallops

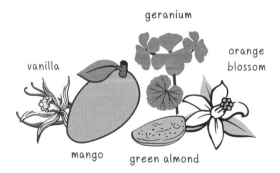

SECONDARY AROMAS

Look for summer-harvested Darjeeling and Nepal teas, labeled "musk" or "muscatel," and the name of the plantation if the tea comes from a single known source.

HIMALAYAN "MUSCATEL"

"Muscatel" refers to a tea whose aromatic bouquet evokes the fruity smoothness of muscat grapes. This exceedingly rare tea owes little to the grower's expertise, the terroir, or even the tea variety. Credit goes to an insect, the leafhopper. This species is related to the insects that attack some Taiwanese oolongs (see page 137), and it causes the same transformations in the tea plant's leaves, producing their unique fragrance.

BLACK TEA ✳ INDIA (DARJEELING) AND NEPAL (DHANKUTA, ILAM) HARVESTED MAY–JUNE

PREPARATION

With a tasting set: 4 minutes in 185°F/85°C water

In a 10-ounce/300 ml teapot: 4 to 5 teaspoons/8 to 10 g of tea in 185°F/85°C water for 4 to 5 minutes

AROMATIC PROFILE

Profile: woodsy/fruity

Color of the liquor: coppery

Astringency: mild astringency

Taste: mild acidity and bitterness

rose · honey · Muscat grapes · resinous wood · mirabelle

DOMINANT AROMAS

SUGGESTED PAIRING

Delicious with white meat or poultry

geranium · coffee beans · vanilla · blackberry

SECONDARY AROMAS

Look for this tea under the name of the plantation if it comes from a single known source. ↓

ASSAM OP TEAS (WHOLE LEAVES)

Assam teas appeal to the so-called British taste. They are vigorous, spicy, tannic, and astringent, well suited to a generous splash of milk. These teas are easily recognized by their golden liquor. They follow the same grading system as the one used in Darjeeling and Sri Lanka (OP, BOP, FOP; see pages 88–89).

BLACK TEA ✳ INDIA (ASSAM) ✳ HARVESTED MAY–JUNE

PREPARATION

With a tasting set: 4 minutes in 203°F/95°C water

In a 10-ounce/300 ml teapot: 4 to 5 teaspoons/8 to 10 g of tea in 203°F/95°C water for 4 minutes

AROMATIC PROFILE

Profile: honeyed/woodsy/spicy

Color of the liquor: coppery

Astringency: marked astringency

Taste: mild bitterness

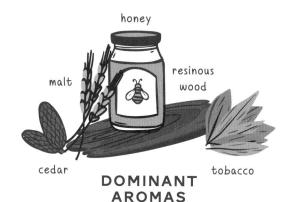

honey

malt

resinous wood

cedar

tobacco

DOMINANT AROMAS

SUGGESTED PAIRING

Delicious with blue cheese

green apple

fruit compote

cinnamon

pear

vanilla

SECONDARY AROMAS

Look for Grand Yunnan Imperial, Yunnan Buds, Yunnan Gold Tips, and Dian Hong Gong Fu.

YUNNAN BLACK TEA

Yunnan's black tea is known as the "surgeon's special," because it provides stimulation without causing jitteriness. It is considered one of China's very best black teas, along with Qimen. It is very aromatic, with little bitterness, and is accessible and available in a variety of grades, depending on the delicacy of the leaf and the quantity of buds. The very best of these teas are known as Yunnan Buds.

BLACK TEA ✱ CHINA (YUNNAN) ✱ HARVESTED MARCH THROUGH NOVEMBER

PREPARATION

With a tasting set: 4 minutes in 185°F/85°C water

In a 10-ounce/300 ml teapot: 4 to 5 teaspoons/8 to 10 g of tea in 185°F/85°C water for 3 to 4 minutes

AROMATIC PROFILE

Profile: woodsy/honeyed

Color of the liquor: brown

Astringency: mildly astringent

Taste: neutral

honey

resinous wood

vanilla

DOMINANT AROMAS

SUGGESTED PAIRING

Delicious with roast beef or game

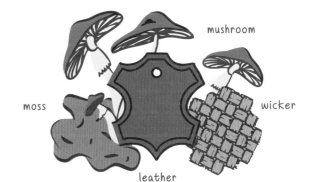

mushroom

moss

wicker

leather

SECONDARY AROMAS

143

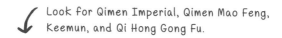
Look for Qimen Imperial, Qimen Mao Feng, Keemun, and Qi Hong Gong Fu.

CHINESE QIMEN

Qimen, a small town in the province of Anhui located south of Mount Huang Shan ("Yellow Mountain"), is famed for its green teas. The production of black tea began here in the 1880s, preceding its cultivation in Yunnan. Quimen teas have a unique aromatic bouquet with a blend of delicious animal notes.

BLACK TEA ✳ CHINA (ANHUI) ✳ HARVESTED MAY–AUGUST

PREPARATION

With a tasting set: 4 minutes in 185°F/85°C water

In a 10-ounce/300 ml teapot: 4 to 5 teaspoons/8 to 10 g in 185°F/85°C water for 3 to 5 minutes

AROMATIC PROFILE

Profile: woodsy/chocolaty

Color of the liquor: coppery

Astringency: subtle astringency

Taste: neutral

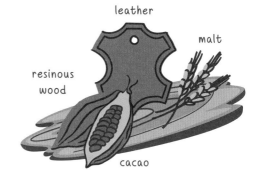

leather

malt

resinous wood

cacao

DOMINANT AROMAS

SUGGESTED PAIRING

Delicious with any chocolate dessert

fruit compote

vanilla

sandalwood

cedar

SECONDARY AROMAS

SOUTH KOREAN JUKRO

Jukro, Korea's only black tea, is a thoroughgoing exception to the rest of the country's production. It is the creation of a brilliant and committed grower, Cho Yun-Seok, who comes from a long line of tea cultivators. Eager to experiment outside traditional parameters, he began to produce black tea ten years ago. The experiment was a resounding success: Jukro is now considered among the finest black teas in the world.

BLACK TEA ✳ SOUTH KOREA (HADONG) ✳ HARVESTED IN MAY

PREPARATION

With a tasting set: 4 minutes in 185°F/85°C water

In a 10-ounce/300 ml teapot: 3 to 4 teaspoons/6 to 8 g of tea in 194°F/90°C water for 4 minutes

AROMATIC PROFILE

Profile: milky/chocolaty

Color of the liquor: coppery

Astringency: no astringency

Taste: mildly sweet

honey
milk
cocoa
vanilla

DOMINANT AROMAS

SUGGESTED PAIRING

Delicious with red berry desserts

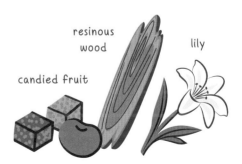

resinous wood
candied fruit
lily

SECONDARY AROMAS

Look for the name of the plantation if
the tea comes from a single known source.

SRI LANKAN BLACK TEA
FBOPFEXS

*Determined to improve the quality of their teas, some Sri Lankan growers realized
that many of the world's tea lovers prefer the beverage without added milk.
They saw the potential of focusing their production on less powerful but more aromatic teas
than those grown in the island's more mountainous areas. This was the origin
of the legendary Flowery Broken Orange Pekoe Finest Extra Special, a new grade that
was enthusiastically received by the export market.*

BLACK TEA ✳ SRI LANKA (LOW-GROWN REGIONS)
HARVESTED MAY–NOVEMBER, DEPENDING ON THE ALTITUDE

PREPARATION

With a tasting set: 3 minutes in
185°F/85°C water

In a 10-ounce/300 ml teapot:
4 to 5 teaspoons/8 to 10 g in
95°C water for 3 minutes

AROMATIC PROFILE

Profile: woodsy/fruity/vanilla

Color of the liquor: mahogany

Astringency: delicate astringency

Taste: a touch of acidity and mild
bitterness

**DOMINANT
AROMAS**

honey

resinous
wood

vanilla

SUGGESTED PAIRING

Delicious with lamb

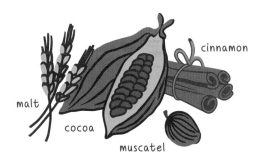

cinnamon

malt

cocoa

muscatel

**SECONDARY
AROMAS**

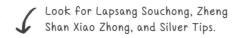

Look for Lapsang Souchong, Zheng Shan Xiao Zhong, and Silver Tips.

SMOKED BLACK TEA FROM FUJIAN

This smoked tea is famed worldwide and is all too often considered the definitive Chinese tea. It can be classified in various ways—quality of the harvest, degree of smokiness—but the natural aromatic components in the leaves are always obliterated. It's no surprise that this tea is usually made from the plant's lower leaves ("souchong"), which produce a tea that is low in caffeine.

BLACK TEA ✳ CHINA (FUJIAN) ✳ HARVESTED APRIL THROUGH NOVEMBER

PREPARATION

In a tasting set: 4 minutes in 203°F/95°C water

In a 10-ounce/300 ml teapot: 4 to 5 teaspoons/8 to 10 g of tea in 203°F/95°C water for 3 to 5 minutes

AROMATIC PROFILE

Profile: smoky

Color of the liquor: amber

Astringency: no astringency

Taste: mild bitterness

bacon

tar

burnt wood

DOMINANT AROMAS

SUGGESTED PAIRING

Delicious with a savory brunch

patchouli

humus

moss

camphor

SECONDARY AROMAS

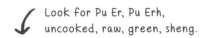
Look for Pu Er, Pu Erh, uncooked, raw, green, sheng.

VINTAGE DARK TEAS

This is the "true" Pu Erh sought by purists. It is prepared traditionally, made from green tea that is naturally fermented to become what the Chinese refer to as "black tea."
It is always compressed and must be aged for at least five years under controlled conditions.
The aging process eliminates the tea's astringency and metallic taste.
It is found only in China.

RAW DARK TEA ✳ CHINA (YUNNAN) ✳ PRESERVED AND "CAVE" AGED

PREPARATION

With a tasting set: 4 minutes in 203°F/95°C water

Gong Fu Cha method: 5 to 10 successive infusions for about 30 seconds in 203°F/95°C water

AROMATIC PROFILE

Profile: woodsy/earthy

Color of the liquor: almost black

Astringency: no astringency

Taste: mild sweetness

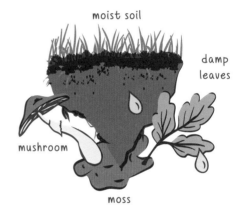

moist soil

damp leaves

mushroom

moss

DOMINANT AROMAS

SUGGESTED PAIRING

Delicious with sautéed mushrooms

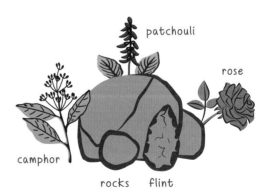

patchouli

rose

camphor

rocks   flint

SECONDARY AROMAS

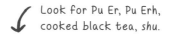

Look for Pu Er, Pu Erh,
cooked black tea, shu.

COOKED DARK TEA

Cooked dark tea is a very recent development, introduced in China in the early 1970s. The initial objective was to accelerate the postfermentation process that occurs naturally in the cakes of green tea. This new approach creates woodsy, powerful teas that natural aging would take decades to accomplish. Although they are primarily made in China, cooked dark teas are now also produced in Laos, Vietnam, and Malawi.

**COOKED DARK TEA ✳ CHINA (YUNNAN), LAOS, VIETNAM, AND MALAWI
HARVESTED YEAR-ROUND**

PREPARATION

In a tasting set: 4 minutes in 203°F/95°C water

Gong Fu Cha method: 5 to 10 successive infusions of about 30 seconds in 203°F/95°C water

AROMATIC PROFILE

Profile: woodsy/animal

Color of the liquor: red

Astringency: delicate astringency

Taste: mildly sweet

SUGGESTED PAIRING

Delicious with aged parmesan or a vieux comté

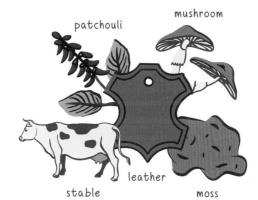

patchouli

mushroom

leather

stable

moss

DOMINANT AROMAS

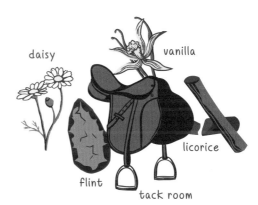

daisy

vanilla

flint

licorice

tack room

SECONDARY AROMAS

PAIRING
TEAS AND
FOODS

WHY PAIR TEAS AND FOODS?

It would be a shame to limit your enjoyment of tea. Why restrict it to a breakfast beverage or an afternoon refreshment, when it's also the ideal accompaniment to a meal?

A GOURMET PRODUCT

Tea is an eminently suitable accompaniment to a meal and complements the most refined dishes.

In the last few years, we have begun to see tasting menus built around skillful pairings of teas and foods, devised by some of the world's greatest chefs. The guiding principle is to match each dish with the tea that best enhances its flavors. Sometimes the combinations play on shared tasting notes, emphasizing the complementarity of flavors. Others create a sharp contrast with disparate aromatic notes that are nevertheless in perfect harmony. Tea has gradually come to play a unique role in cuisine.

TEA OR WINE?

Tea is an excellent alternative to wine. It is favored by knowledgeable diners who wish to limit their alcohol consumption, particularly at business luncheons.

The issue of pairing wine with food has been a hotly debated and integral aspect of gastronomy for decades. **Tea, on the other hand, was long consigned to pairings with Asian dishes, and often occupied a distinct and** **subordinate spot** apart from the inevitable wine list.

Tea is also often associated with light dishes and considered unworthy of accompanying the classic recipes of French cuisine.

But tea is actually the only beverage that offers a diversity of flavors and bouquets comparable to those of wine. Try to go beyond accepted (and often outdated) preconceptions and explore new culinary horizons. It's intriguing to envision each match by recognizing the vast variety of teas, the multiplicity of their flavors, and the range of tasting temperatures. You'll find yourself imagining an almost infinite number of potential pairings.

A TIME-HONORED TRADITION IN CHINA AND JAPAN

It's impossible to imagine a dinner in China or Japan where a guest is not offered tea immediately upon being seated. It might be a jasmine variety, or perhaps a green tea, usually roasted. You can rest assured that your cup will be assiduously refilled throughout the meal.

ASIAN TRADITIONS

In Japan, the roasted fragrance of a Hojicha or the toasty notes of a Genmaicha have a well-established place at the table, pairing naturally and seamlessly with Japanese cuisine. These teas make such dishes as tempura or broiled eel more digestible. High-quality sashimi is always accompanied by a fine green tea in traditional restaurants.

The blended iodine, grassy, and sometimes fruity notes of a Japanese green tea are unsurpassed for accompanying raw fish dishes.

In China, tea is of course served with every meal, whatever the time of day or evening, but it's also an excuse for a meal in its own right. When you visit a teahouse, you can order a selection of small dishes to accompany your tasting.

In these countries, tea is a constant presence on every occasion throughout the day, hailed for its many benefits—it hydrates the system, helps the digestion of oily foods, and warms the body.

IT'S NO LONGER LIMITED TO AFTERNOON TEA

The British have invited tea to the table, **for brunch** and afternoon enjoyment as well as breakfast. Smoked teas go well with such selections as scrambled eggs, bacon, and sausages, acting as the perfect foil to their savory flavors. **Brunch is a meal in its own right** that includes both sweet and savory nibbles—mini-sandwiches, muffins, scones—most often accompanied by an Earl Grey.

A LITTLE HISTORY

The ritual of afternoon tea originated around 1840 in the salon of the Duchess of Bedford. She inaugurated the custom of inviting friends to gather for tea and cakes in the afternoon, and this pleasant interlude became a ritual. The broader adoption of afternoon tea also reflected the impact of the Industrial Revolution's rhythm and pace of the working day. A later dinner necessitated a rejuvenating pause in the day's activities.

THE ADVANTAGES OF TEA OVER WINE

Tea is winning more and more converts as the beverage of choice with midday meals during the week—business luncheons, for example. It's an appealing alternative that offers an array of sometimes unrecognized benefits.

TEA VS. WINE: THE FACEOFF

Although some diners may have doubts about tea as an alternative to wine, the case for tea is strong.

Tea is attracting new aficionados who care about their health and well-being.

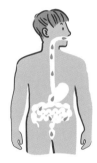

Tea promotes hydration and improves digestion.

Tea doesn't impair judgment.

Tea can be consumed in unlimited quantities at any age.

Tea is adaptable to an infinite number of food pairings.

Tea's temperature can be adjusted to bring out the best in individual foods, adding to their textural appeal and helping them melt deliciously in the mouth.

Tea is a refreshing and imaginative alternative to alcoholic drinks.

Tea aids mental focus and concentration.

Tea is economical.

A word to the wise: It takes a certain degree of organization and initiative to follow the instructions on the proper serving temperature for each tea. Allow a little extra time if you want to create outstanding pairings.

A DISH, A TEA, A WINE

Fine-dining establishments have accustomed us to the time-honored duo of one dish/one wine, orchestrated by the sommelier. But why not extend and enhance the gustatory experience by pairing each dish with a tea as well as a wine, doubling the diner's pleasure?

A THREESOME IS BEST

This little ménage à trois experiment helps you savor each food to the maximum. Take a sip of either wine or tea, alternating with every mouthful.

You'll find you have a different impression of the dish, depending on the beverage that accompanies it. You can compare the different harmonies created as well as the advantages of each of the pairings.

This experiment enriches the tasting experience, opens new possibilities, and offers many opportunities for exploration, whether you're dining in restaurants or at home.

When consumed along with wine during a meal, tea has the advantage of providing hydration, facilitating digestion, and reducing the sensation of dryness that the tannins in some wines leave in the mouth.

As a member of this trio, tea allows you to leave the table without a sensation of heaviness, even though you'll have enjoyed a very rich gastronomic experience. It thus proves itself to be an indispensable culinary ally.

WHAT MAKES FOR A GOOD PAIRING?

A good pairing is a marriage that brings out the best in both partners. The tea should pay homage to the dish, and the dish should bring out the best in the tea. A successful alliance is usually perfectly obvious. Just tell yourself that it's not complicated, it goes without saying, it's completely intuitive... and you'll make the right choice.

CRITERIA FOR CHOOSING

For an ideal match, consider the textures, aromas, and flavors of the recipe, and select your tea based on these criteria. **Is the dish you've ordered rather rich and heavy? What are its main ingredients?**

The flavor notes of the food and teas should complement and enhance each other.

CARRY OUT AN INVESTIGATION

Let's take an example: creating the ideal pairing between a tea and a honey madeleine. You should consider the rich texture of the madeleine and its buttery, toasty, vanilla, and honeyed flavors, seeking out the tea that will bring all these tastes to the fore.

Carry out a similar analysis, whether you're pondering the best accompaniment for a duck breast or a raspberry tart.

FOOD AND TEA, TEA AND FOOD

You can also start by selecting one of your favorite teas and asking yourself what type of food would go best with it, deciding what dishes would be most likely to bring out its distinctive qualities.

RULES FOR A HAPPY MARRIAGE

Depending on the effect you desire, there are three distinct approaches to exploring the ideal pairing of tea with food. The objective is always the same: the creation of gustatory harmony. You can toy with tone on tone nuances, dream up a harmonious blend, or highlight flavor contrasts.

🔴🔴 TONE ON TONE

This approach seeks out points of resemblance between the tea and the food you are matching. For example, you might pair a honey madeleine with a creamy-textured tea, whose liquor gives an impression of richness with buttery, vanilla, and honeyed notes. Try a Taiwanese oolong (ideally a Dong Ding).

🔴⚫ CONTRAST

This approach to pairing aims at defying expectations and confronting two very distinct personalities, while ultimately seeking harmony. The idea is to combine teas and foods with contrasting but compatible qualities. Returning to our example of the honey madeleine, a Da Hong Pao, with its powerful aromas of coffee grounds, prunes, and dry wood, will contrast with the madeleine, emphasizing its honeyed notes and the warm mellowness of its buttery flavors.

🔴⚪ FUSION

This harmony is obtained by combining two distinct impressions. For example, if you sip an Earl Grey at the same time you nibble a honey madeleine, the flavors will blend together in your mouth. Honey on the one hand and bergamot on the other provide gentle citrus notes, recalling the lively fragrance of orange zest.

AS AN APERITIF

Serving tea as an aperitif—now, that's a bright idea! It hydrates your body, stimulates your taste buds, and heightens anticipation for the delicacies that await.

WITH TAPAS

A multifaceted tea, such as a Chinese Dan Cong, is an excellent accompaniment to a variety of tapas. This grand cru tea has a lingering after-taste and an exceptional aromatic palate that plays off against the tapas and makes the most of their stimulating contrasts.

Infuse at: 194°F/90°C
Serve at: 86°F/30°C

WITH A CHARCUTERIE PLATTER

Lapsang Souchong's powerful flavors and smoky notes will exhilarate your taste buds and give you a radically new perception of that array of various cured meats and sausages.

Infuse at: 194°F/90°C
Serve at: 86°F/30°C

WITH FOIE GRAS

Aromatically rich Yunnan Buds tea features the same animal and honeyed notes as foie gras. The marriage of flavors produces a delightfully lingering aftertaste.

Infuse at: room temperature
Serve at: 68° to 86°F/20° to 30°C

or

Consider a Dong Ding from Taiwan, with its floral, buttery, vanilla, and grassy notes. It's a match that's just as delicious as the classic foie gras–Gewürztraminer pairing.

Infuse at: 194°F/90°C
Serve at: 68° to 86°F/20° to 30°C

WITH CAVIAR

Choose one of the finest Japanese spring-harvest teas to accent the distinctive iodine notes of both the caviar and the beverage accompanying it.

Infuse at: room temperature
Serve at: 68° to 86°F/20° to 30°C

 Tone on tone   Contrast   Fusion

STYLISH SERVICE IN A GLASS

⋈

Serving tea in a glass designed for alcoholic drinks provides unexpected pleasures. Choose from the vast range of custom-designed glassware to select the format that will best complement the tea's color and aromas. Try:

✳ ***A vodka glass*** *for a perfectly clear tea*

✳ ***A brandy snifter*** *that can be slowly swirled to bring out woodsy aromas*

✳ ***A cordial glass*** *whose small size will emphasize the delicacy of the liquor*

Once again, the world of wine and spirits is an inexhaustible source of inspiration for tea connoisseurs. Choose a glass designed for wine, cordials, or vodka. Feel free to experiment with the best way to present imaginative pairings of tea and food!

WITH THE FIRST COURSE

Presented with the first course, tea opens the meal with an agreeably light and subtle note.
It's a welcome novelty, guaranteed to offer your guests a pleasant surprise.

WITH A CHILLED VEGETABLE VELOUTÉ

Try the tone-on-tone approach with a lightly oxidized Taiwanese oolong, whose vivid green hue will accent the vegetables' freshness.

Infuse at: 194°F/90°C
Serve at: 68° to 86°F/20° to 30°C

WITH CRAB OR LOBSTER RAVIOLI

Select a "stem" tea, such as Shiraore Kuki Hojicha, for a surprise pairing that contrasts the tea's toasty vanilla flavor with the iodine notes of the ravioli.

Infuse at: 194°F/90°C
Serve at: 122°F/50°C

WITH POACHED EGGS IN RED WINE SAUCE

With its delicate astringency, the intensely mineral and grassy notes of a Chinese spring-harvest green tea offer a sense of freshness that lingers in the mouth. Its zesty edge plays off against the deeper aromas of the red wine sauce.

Infuse at: 176°F/80°C
Serve at: 104°F/40°C

WITH A SAUTÉ OF MUSHROOMS

A vintage Pu Erh with a woodsy bouquet will bring out the flavor of the mushrooms. You'll experience new dimensions of this dish and relish its savory similarities with the tea.

Infuse at: 194°F/90°C
Serve at: 104°F/40°C

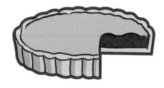

WITH A VEGETABLE TART OR A QUICHE LORRAINE

The woodsy fragrance of a deeply oxidized Taiwanese oolong contrasts splendidly with the aromas of golden pastry, while also offering an appealing sensation of lightness.

Infuse at: 194°F/90°C
Serve at: 86°F/30°C

WITH MEAT

Be bold, and invite tea to join your table! You'll experience the remarkable harmonies of black teas matched with red or white meats and poultry. Whether structured or round, from China or India, teas are a delicious counterpoint to meats, very much like fine red wines.

WITH ROASTED OR GRILLED BEEF

The finest Yunnan black teas make for a revelatory pairing. The notes of leather, honey, and tobacco meld with the rich browned aromas of roasted or grilled meats.

Infuse at: 194°F/90°C
Serve at: 104°F/40°C

WITH WHITE MEAT (VEAL, PORK) OR POULTRY

Structured teas with spicy or fruity flavors, such as summer-harvested Darjeelings, Assams, or Yunnans, are ideal. They enhance the flavors of these delicate meats without overwhelming them.

Infuse at: 185°F/85°C
Serve at: 104°F/40°C

WITH LAMB

Yunnan's black teas or fine Sri Lankan varieties are good accompaniments. Their notes of leather and honey emphasize the flavor of the lamb, which in turn tempers and refines the tannins of the tea.

Infuse at: 194°F/90°C
Serve at: 104°F/40°C

WITH SQUAB OR DUCK

Select black Yunnan teas for their remarkable honey fragrance to create a perfect match with these savory poultry dishes.

Infuse at: 194°F/90°C
Serve at: 104°F/40°C

WITH GAME BIRDS AND MEATS

To stand up against the powerful flavors of game dishes, select a Pu Erh or a Yunnan black tea with an assertive personality.

Infuse at: 194°F/90°C
Serve at: 104°F/40°C

 Tone on tone   Contrast   Fusion

WITH FISH, CRUSTACEANS, AND SHELLFISH

There's a good reason that tea traditionally accompanies sushi in Japan.
Green tea pairs beautifully with anything that comes from the sea.
It respects the delicate flavor of these foods, and its iodized notes make the perfect pairing.

WITH RAW FISH

Japanese green teas with strong iodine notes, such as most Senchas, accent the matching notes in the fish.

Infuse at: 140°F/60°C
Serve at: 68° to 86°F/20° to 30°C

WITH COOKED FISH

To go with a grilled fish (snapper, sea bream, or sea bass, for example), try a Japanese green tea with intense iodine and grassy notes that has a creamy mouth feel. Consider a Ryokucha Midori.

Infuse at: 140°F/60°C
Serve at: 104°F/40°C

or

The velvety texture of a Japanese Tamaryokucha tea pairs perfectly with steamed or smoked fish. The buttery, marine aromas of the tea are the perfect complement to the flavors of the fish.

Infuse at: 167°F/75°C
Serve at: 104°F/40°C

WITH GRILLED OR SMOKED FISH (SALMON, HERRING, TROUT, ETC.)

A Bancha Hojicha's woodsy and grilled flavors go very well with the powerful animal notes of the fish. Tea also helps to hydrate the body, a distinct advantage when serving fish recipes that can make you thirsty.

Infuse at: 194°F/90°C
Serve at: 122°F/50°C

 Tone on tone   Contrast   Fusion

WITH CRUSTACEANS

Experiment with matching a Bancha Hojicha, whose appealing fruity, woodsy bouquet harmoniously accompanies the iodine notes of lobster, crab, and other crustaceans.

Infuse at: 194°F/90°C
Serve at: 68° to 86°F/20° to 30°C

WITH SHELLFISH WITH INTENSE IODINE OVERTONES (OYSTERS, CLAMS, ETC.)

Japanese green teas with strong iodine notes, such as most Senchas, will boost and enhance the distinctive marine flavors of the mollusks.

Infuse at: 140°F/60°C
Serve at: 68° to 86°F/20° to 30°C

WITH SCALLOPS

Try an AV2 spring-harvest Darjeeling, whose subtle texture and roselike aromas will contribute richness to the shellfish dish without overwhelming its delicate flavor.

Infuse at: 185°F/85°C
Serve at: 104°F/40°C

WITH PASTA, LASAGNA, OR RISOTTO

Pasta, risottos, and their countless iterations are best matched with a tea that echoes the dominant flavors of the recipe. If tea is used as one of the ingredients (as a poaching liquid, for example), it should be served as the accompanying beverage.

 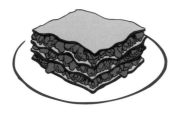 

WITH TAGLIATELLE WITH LEMON AND BASIL

A green tea scented with yuzu complements the basil and lemon flavors. The intensely grassy green tea and zesty yuzu meld harmoniously with the tart, herbal flavors of the pasta sauce.

Infuse at: 158°F/70°C
Serve at: 86°F/30°C

WITH TOMATO-BASED PASTA DISHES AND LASAGNA

The freshness of a spring-harvest Darjeeling is the perfect foil for the tomato flavor, enhancing its appealing acidity.

Infuse at: 185°F/85°C
Serve at: 104°F/40°C

WITH WALNUT AND GORGONZOLA SAUCED PASTA

The woodsy notes of a Taiwanese oxidized oolong, such as Butterfly of Taiwan, create a welcome contrast to the animal and milky notes of the cheese and accent the nutty overtones of the dish.

Infuse at: 194°F/90°C
Serve at: 104°F/40°C

WITH SPECIALTY PASTA DISHES

Try a tone-on-tone match with a green tea, such as a Genmaicha, made with tasty grains of popped brown rice.

Infuse at: 167°F/75°C
Serve at: 104°F/40°C

WITH RISOTTO ALLA MILANESE

Try Genmaicha with this dish, too. The Japanese green tea, enhanced with popped brown rice, gives a tip of its cap to the risotto.

Infuse at: 167°F/75°C
Serve at: 104°F/40°C

WITH A MUSHROOM OR TRUFFLE RISOTTO

A Yunnan Buds tea will work wonders. This Chinese black tea has resinous wood and honey notes. Redolent of forest floor, moss, and mushrooms, the tea resonates beautifully with the flavors of this risotto.

Infuse at: 194°F/90°C
Serve at: 104°F/40°C

WITH A SEAFOOD RISOTTO

There's no better match for seafood than a Japanese green tea with strong iodine notes. Try an Imperial Tamaryokucha.

Infuse at: 167°F/75°C
Serve at: 104°F/40°C

 Tone on tone   Contrast   Fusion

WITH CHEESE

*If ever there was a gustatory realm where wine claims supremacy, it's surely the domain of cheese!
But teas are worthy challengers. Their wealth of aromas makes it easy to determine
the appropriate tea for every imaginable cheese. And sipped warm, tea allows the cheese's aromas
to fully express themselves. The texture of a cheese is also a defining criterion, because it conveys
the robustness of a tea or reveals its subtlety.*

WITH A NATURAL OR WASHED-RIND SOFT CHEESE (CAMEMBERT, BRIE, SAINT-MARCELLIN, PONT-L'ÉVEQUE)

A Bancha Hojicha is the very best choice. When sipped with the cheese, it develops a very mellow bouquet of dried and preserved fruits with hazelnut notes.

Infuse at: 68°F/20°C
Serve at: 68°F/20°C

WITH A SHEEP'S MILK CHEESE

Deeply oxidized Taiwanese oolongs with fruity, woodsy, honeyed notes harmonize perfectly with these cheeses. The tea gains complexity, and the cheese becomes longer in the mouth.

Infuse at: 68°F/20°C
Serve at: 68°F/20°C

WITH A BLUE CHEESE (ROQUEFORT, GORGONZOLA, ETC.)

Strong, spicy teas, such as Qimen, Assam, or Sichuan black teas, are good choices. Their notes of leather, pepper, and fruit blend seamlessly with intense blue cheese flavors.

Infuse at: 68°F/20°C
Serve at: 68°F/20°C

WITH PARMESAN

Select a dark tea, such as a Pu Erh, that will take the edge off the cheese's saltiness while enhancing its distinctive flavor.

Infuse at: 68°F/20°C
Serve at: 68°F/20°C

WITH A GOAT CHEESE

Chinese green teas are very good choices. Their grassy, mineral notes are heightened by the cheese, whose flavors are enhanced by the pairing.

Infuse at: 68°F/20°C
Serve at: 68°F/20°C

WITH A FIRM-COOKED CURD CHEESE (COMTÉ, BEAUFORT, GRUYÈRE)

Try either a Pu Erh or a summer Darjeeling, both of which would go admirably with the fruity notes of the cheese. The graininess of aged comtés mitigates the tea's astringency

Infuse at: 68°F/20°C
Serve at: 68°F/20°C

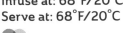

WITH SWEET TREATS

It's traditional to brew a cup of tea to go with an afternoon snack, and it doesn't take much imagination to think up good nibbles to accompany it. Make sure that tea has a place of honor at your afternoon break!

WITH FINANCIERS (ALMOND CAKES)

Choose a moderately oxidized Taiwanese tea (Dong Ding, Jin Xuan) that pairs beautifully with almond flavors. You'll find that the financier accents the floral notes of the tea.

Infuse at: 194°F/90°C
Serve at: 104°F/40°C

or

Many lovely jasmine teas lend themselves perfectly to this pairing. Nibble on a financier while sipping one of these teas. You'll find the cake tastes richer and fresher, and the tea's floral notes will blossom.

Infuse at: 167°F/75°C
Serve at: 104°F/40°C

WITH MATCHA MADELEINES

Japanese green Sencha teas are very best friends with these little delicacies that are perfumed with matcha. They contribute a grassy note that's agreeably long in the mouth.

Infuse at: 158°F/70°C
Serve at: 104°F/40°C

WITH FRUITCAKE

Deeply oxidized Taiwanese teas allow the flavors and fragrances of the fruits, too often obscured in the cake, to reemerge for your enjoyment.

Infuse at: 194°F/90°C
Serve at: 104°F/40°C

WITH FRUIT MUFFINS (FIG, DRIED APRICOT)

Consider a summer-harvested Darjeeling or Nepal for mutual flavor enhancement. The notes of honey and dried fruits in the muffins reinforce the flavors of the tea, and vice versa.

Infuse at: 185°F/85°C
Serve at: 104°F/40°C

 Tone on tone   Contrast   Fusion

WITH DESSERT

*Western cooks have long understood that sweet flavors and tea are natural companions,
so it's no surprise that tea is so frequently served with desserts.
Here are a few classic combinations for you to enjoy.*

WITH A LEMON TART

Try the tone-on-tone approach with an Earl Grey, whose bergamot notes give a boost to the zesty filling of the pastry in a spirit of mutual cooperation.

Infuse at: 194°F/90°C
Serve at: 104°F/40°C

WITH A RED BERRY DESSERT

The range of choices is as broad as the variety of red fruits. They lend themselves to numerous pairings, whether served in desserts, pastries, or sorbets. Fine jasmine teas are set off by raspberry; fruity, woodsy teas, such as deeply oxidized oolongs and Bancha Hojichas, provide an intriguing counter-point to the lively flavors of red fruits. If you're looking for a Black Forest Cake effect, try a tea with chocolaty notes—a Qimen or a Jukro, for example.

Infuse at: 194°F/90°C
Serve at: 86°F/30°C

WITH A CRÈME CARAMEL

Enjoy the light texture of a mildly oxidized oolong, such as Dong Ding, Bao Zhong, or Huang Jing Gui. The vanilla scented sweetness of the custard is enhanced by the tea's grassy, floral notes.

Infuse at: 194°F/90°C
Serve at: 104°F/40°C

WITH A TARTE TATIN

A deeply oxidized Taiwanese oolong with a woodsy, spiced fruit bouquet melds perfectly with the tart's meltingly soft apple filling.

Infuse at: 194°F/90°C
Serve at: 104°F/40°C

WITH FRESH FRUITS OR A FRUIT SALAD

It's not easy to find the right pairing for a Chinese white tea, but its subtle, respectful harmonies are welcome with fresh fruit. For a more emphatic flavor, you might consider a lightly oxidized oolong (Bao Zhong, Anxi Tie Guan Yin) that will lend a floral, grassy vivacity to the fruits.

Infuse at: 194°F/90°C
Serve at: 68°F/20°C

WITH CHOCOLATE

Chocolate begins to melt at 96.8°F/36°C. As tea warms the interior of the mouth, it releases an explosion of chocolate flavors, whether tasted on their own or combined with other ingredients. The aromas of chocolate mingle with those of tea to create an opulent gustatory experience.

QIMEN TEAS

This family of teas is characterized by notes of cocoa and malt that give a boost to chocolate flavors.

Infuse at: 194°F/90°C
Serve at: 104°F/40°C

DEEPLY OXIDIZED TAIWANESE OOLONGS

The woodsy notes of these teas offer a powerful counterpoint to chocolate's floral, honeyed, sweet notes.

Infuse at: 194°F/90°C
Serve at: 104°F/40°C

SOUTH KOREAN JUKRO

There's an incredible tone-on-tone effect created by this most chocolaty-tasting of teas. If you serve Jukro with a bittersweet chocolate cake, for example, the tea accentuates the dessert's notes of cacao and butter. In turn, the tea's flavors gain fullness and length in the mouth.

Infuse at: 194°F/90°C
Serve at: 104°F/40°C

VARIOUS CITRUS-FLAVORED TEAS

Try one of these for a fresh and lively pairing that balances the spicy notes of cacao.

Infuse at: 194°F/90°C
Serve at: 104°F/40°C

ELEGANT JASMINE TEAS

Tasted together, the cacao in the chocolate becomes sweeter and milkier, enhanced by the jasmine tea's floral notes.

Infuse at: 167°F/75°C
Serve at: 104°F/40°C

 Tone on tone   Contrast   Fusion

COOKING
WITH TEA

TEA STARTED OUT AS A FOOD

*Tea has been consumed for over 3,000 years,
initially as a recipe ingredient rather than as a drink. In China, tea was originally grown
to be added to a soup, not to be infused as a beverage.*

THERE'S TEA IN MY SOUP!

The *Shijing* ("Book of Songs"), written in the eighth century BC, alludes to the use of tea leaves, classified as bitter herbs, in cooking.

For a long time, tea was an ingredient in soup, along with spices, onions, salt, and occasionally flowers, It was compressed into bricks that were roasted before being crumbled and mixed into boiling water. This is the way tea is still consumed in some regions of Tibet.

TEA ASSUMES A PLACE OF HONOR

Around AD 1000, during the Chinese Song Dynasty, tea assumed a more elevated status. It was no longer just one ingredient among many in a simple soup recipe—it had earned respect in its own right. Tea leaves were now pulverized into a fine powder to be blended with simmering water.

The preparation of Matcha in the Japanese Cha No Yu ceremony (see pages 64–65) corresponds exactly to this mode of consumption. It's only in the last 500 to 600 years, following practices introduced during the Chinese Ming Dynasty (1368–1644), that we've been immersing the leaves in hot water and then straining them out of the infusion.

THREE GOLDEN RULES

Tea can be used as an ingredient in all its forms, whether as whole dry leaves, pulverized in a food mill, or infused in liquid (liquor). The liquor may sometimes be brewed extra strong to obtain a tea extract that is more powerful than what we customarily drink as a beverage. But before playing with all the possible iterations, let's review three fundamental golden rules for cooking with tea.

GOLDEN RULE I

Substitute tea for water whenever possible.

✖

Every time water or another liquid is called for in a recipe, consider tea as a subtle and savory alternative. Rice and vegetables are usually tastier when cooked in a spiced tea. You might deglaze a pan after cooking a filet mignon with a Taiwanese oolong. For basting a chicken midway through the cooking time, try adding a Grand Yunnan Imperial to the cooking juices.

GOLDEN RULE II

Water's not the only option for infusing tea.

✖

You can also infuse tea in milk or cream. Adjust the amount of tea and the infusion time, depending on whether you're brewing it in warm or cold liquid. Using tea will introduce novel flavors to creams and emulsions, allowing intriguing fresh takes on some of the great classic recipes of French cuisine.

GOLDEN RULE III

Don't just toss leftover tea.

✖

If you haven't finished the last drop, save the remainder and add it as seasoning to the dish you're preparing for dinner.

Now you're ready to explore. Try these twenty different ways to introduce tea into your culinary repertoire.

IN MY PANTRY

	Eating tea p. 176	Infusing tea in water for a court bouillon p. 177	Infusing tea in water for direct cooking p. 178	Infusing tea in water as a base for soup p. 179	Infusing tea in cream or milk p. 180	Making a bed of tea leaves p. 181	Making a marinade p. 182	Making an aspic p. 183
Japanese green teas	●	●	●		●	●	●	●
Chinese green teas	●	●	●		●	●	●	●
Roasted green teas		●	●	●	●		●	●
Chinese black teas		●	●		●		●	●
Darjeeling		●			●		●	●
Other black teas (Assam, Sri Lanka)		●	●		●		●	●
Dark teas		●	●	●	●		●	●
Lightly oxidized oolongs		●	●		●		●	●
Deeply oxidized oolongs		●	●		●		●	●
Smoked teas		●	●	●	●		●	●
Flavored teas			●	●	●		●	●

Making an emulsion p. 184	Dusting powdered tea p. 185	Reducing p. 186	Deglazing p. 187	Making a salt crust p. 188	Piercing and scoring p. 189	Basting p. 190	Making an extract p. 191	Smoking p. 192	Adding color p. 193

EATING TEA

Tea can sometimes take the place of a vegetable, lending itself to the same cooking and preparation methods. The leaves can be incorporated into salads, tempura, and pickles, or they can be steamed or tossed in a stir-fry.

HOW TO GO ABOUT IT

The leaves must always be rehydrated, and there are two ways to do this:

✳ **rapidly rehydrate the leaves** by soaking them briefly (30 seconds or so) in water at the appropriate temperature. The leaves will retain the maximum degree of flavor and taste, but you may not get the benefit of all these components as you chew the food; some of these aromatic elements require infusion for a specific time and temperature to be released.

✳ **by reusing the leaves** from tea you've already prepared. Try them in salad, tempura, or pickles.

THE GUSTATORY EXPERIENCE

When chewing raw or cooked tea leaves, you'll experience a grassy freshness that lingers pleasantly in the mouth.

THE RIGHT TEA TO CHOOSE

Select young sprouts of spring-harvested green tea: they are tender and their flavor is not too bitter.

Steamed in the Japanese style, their fragrance recalls spinach or watercress.

If you **roast them in the Chinese fashion**, they'll suggest fresh hazelnuts with a touch of astringency.

SHINCHA SALAD WITH BONITO AND SOY SAUCE

In each small dish or bowl, place 3 pinches of tender, fresh Shincha leaves, already infused. Add 2 pinches of dried bonito flakes and 3 drops of artisanal soy sauce. If you wish, scatter a few sesame seeds on top.

Enjoy with chopsticks following a tea tasting.

INFUSING TEA IN WATER FOR A COURT BOUILLON

Tea is a valuable member of the extended family of bouillons and cooking stocks. Use it for adding moisture to recipes, poaching, and serving as a cooking base or a consommé.

HOW TO GO ABOUT IT

Tea can be used in two different ways.

✳ **as one of the ingredients to lend flavor to a bouillon:** you could include tea leaves in a bouquet garni, for example;

✳ **as a bouillon in its own right:** the tea liquor, which may vary in strength, just needs a judicious addition of salt and pepper.

THE GUSTATORY EXPERIENCE

Included in a bouquet garni, tea leaves release fragrances that blend with the other flavors in the bouillon. They offer a touch of novelty, like a spice.

Used as a poaching liquid for fish, chicken, eggs, etc., a tea-based bouillon discreetly communicates its aroma without being overbearing. It's ideal for delicate dishes.

When tasted, the tea bouillon contributes color, flavor, and fragrance.

THE RIGHT TEA TO CHOOSE

If including tea in a bouquet garni, select one that can hold its own with the other ingredients. Try a Chinese black tea or a deeply oxidized oolong.

For a poaching liquid, choose teas that are assertive enough to communicate their taste to the dish you are preparing. Consider a Pu Erh, black, or smoked tea.

To moisten, adding liquid, or for a consommé, any tea may be used, depending on the recipe.

OCHAZUKE (RICE WITH SENCHA)

Half fill a large bowl with cooked rice, preferably a Japanese or Carnaroli variety. Pour in 13.5 ounces/400 ml of warm Sencha green tea. Add a few pieces of grilled salmon and sprinkle with sesame seeds, dried seaweed, and a bit of horseradish. You can use this as a base and add vegetables, mushrooms, and even a few infused Sencha leaves. It's a delicious and invigorating dish.

INFUSING TEA IN WATER FOR DIRECT COOKING (GRAINS AND LEGUMES)

Cereals and grains are important sources of energy and nutrients that are essential for our health. They are prepared by simmering in water or other liquid. Cooking them in tea is a good way to enliven their flavors and add a savory touch.

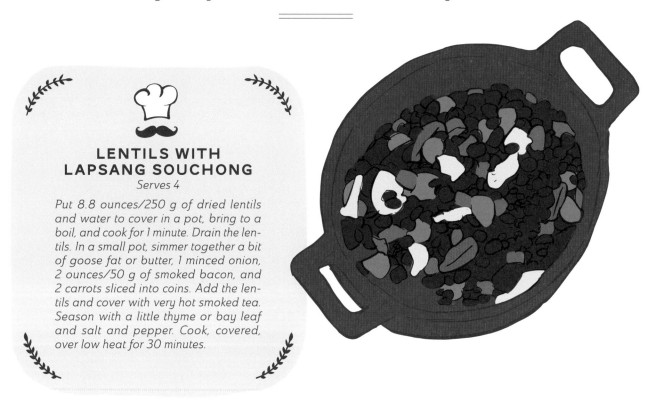

LENTILS WITH LAPSANG SOUCHONG
Serves 4

Put 8.8 ounces/250 g of dried lentils and water to cover in a pot, bring to a boil, and cook for 1 minute. Drain the lentils. In a small pot, simmer together a bit of goose fat or butter, 1 minced onion, 2 ounces/50 g of smoked bacon, and 2 carrots sliced into coins. Add the lentils and cover with very hot smoked tea. Season with a little thyme or bay leaf and salt and pepper. Cook, covered, over low heat for 30 minutes.

HOW TO GO ABOUT IT

You can use tea in two ways:

* **prepare the desired amount in a teapot** and then add it to the recipe;

* **add the tea leaves directly to the pot**, removing them later with a skimmer.

THE GUSTATORY EXPERIENCE

Even if the liquor is quite strong, tea used this way lends a delicate flavor to cooked foods. **Grains, legumes, and pastas** rehydrate and absorb the tea so that the food is permeated by the flavor.

THE BEST TEA TO CHOOSE

Almost any strong tea can be used for this purpose. Consider robust black teas, smoked teas, and spiced teas.

For cooking potatoes, oolongs and certain green teas, such as Japanese Senchas, are good choices.

INFUSING TEA IN WATER
AS A BASE FOR SOUP

Try using tea leaves as you would a spice or condiment.
It's an easy way to add a touch of originality to your soups, stews, and purees.

PUMPKIN VELOUTÉ
WITH EARL GREY
Serves 4

Prepare 16 ounces/500 ml of Earl Grey green tea. Coarsely chop 1 pound/1 kg of fresh pumpkin, 1/2 pound/500 g of carrots, and 2 potatoes. In a pot, sweat 1 minced onion and 1 garlic clove in a bit of olive oil, and sauté the diced vegetables. Add the tea and 16 ounces/500 ml of milk. Salt and pepper to taste. Cook, covered, for 30 minutes. Blend to a puree. Correct the seasoning. Add a splash of cream and season with ground nutmeg or orange zest.

HOW TO
GO ABOUT IT

Add the tea leaves during the last few minutes of cooking the soup, just long enough for them to infuse. Blend the soup, including the leaves.

THE GUSTATORY
EXPERIENCE

Tea brings its aromas and a hint of astringency that lingers in the mouth.

The result will be even more striking **if you use a smoked, roasted, or flavored tea**.

THE BEST TEA
TO CHOOSE

It's best to used smoked, roasted, fired, dark, or spiced or citrus-flavored teas.

INFUSING TEA IN CREAM OR MILK

Just like cooking stock, cream and milk can easily be flavored with tea.
It provides subtle variations in sauces, emulsions, mousses, and other dairy based desserts.

HOW TO GO ABOUT IT

Simply infuse the tea in milk or cream, adjusting the time and temperature as appropriate. The tea will take longer to infuse at room temperature and shorter if the milk or cream is heated.

THE GUSTATORY EXPERIENCE

Tea conveys its aromas, adding flavor to the recipe. The fat content of the cream or milk "sets" even the most delicate tea aromas much more effectively than water. This is a real advantage when you're making desserts with an airy texture, such as mousses, foams, and froths.

THE BEST TEA TO CHOOSE

Any tea can be used, flavored or plain.

CRÈME AU CHAI
Serves 4

Preheat the oven to 195°F/90°C. In a pot, bring 16 ounces/450 ml of whole milk to a boil. Add 1 heaping teaspoon of spiced tea (Chai) and allow to infuse for 4 minutes. Strain. In a large bowl, combine 4 egg yolks, 2.5 ounces/75 g of sugar, and 2.5 g/75 g of thick crème fraîche. Add the flavored milk and whisk vigorously. Pour the mixture into 4 ramekins and bake for 30 to 40 minutes. Let cool to room temperature.

MAKING A BED OF TEA LEAVES

You can "make a bed" of already infused leaves as a base for cooking a fish fillet, adding a grassy nuance to its iodine notes.

HOW TO GO ABOUT IT

Arrange a bed of infused leaves, spreading a layer about 3/8 inch/ 1 cm thick. Place the fish fillet on top. This is a useful technique for steaming foods in general.

THE GUSTATORY EXPERIENCE

The tea's fresh notes of cut grass pair beautifully with the flavors and aromas of the fish.

THE BEST TEA TO CHOOSE

Select a Japanese or Chinese green tea.

BANCHA STEAMED MONKFISH

Preheat the oven to 425°F/210°C. Pour a splash of olive oil onto a piece of parchment paper, sprinkle with 1 tablespoon of green tea (Bancha), and place the monkfish on top. Add a few blanched vegetables (cherry tomatoes, white onion, rounds of cucumber, or zucchini). Salt and pepper to taste. Before sealing the packet, sprinkle with a not-too-dry white wine. Bake for 12 minutes.

MAKING A MARINADE

Marinades add flavor to foods through the process of osmosis. They also tenderize tougher cuts of meat and extend their shelf life. Tea can be incorporated as an additional ingredient to add flavor or serve as the base of the marinating liquid.

HOW TO GO ABOUT IT

✳ **For an uncooked marinade:** replace your recipe's main liquid ingredient with the same quantity of very concentrated tea liquor, or incorporate a generous amount of leaves (a heaping 3 tablespoons/20 g) as an additional ingredient in the marinade.

✳ **For a cooked marinade:** add 5 tablespoons of tea leaves per 1 quart/1 L of marinade.

✳ **For an instant marinade:** grind the tea leaves into a powder and sprinkle them on top of the food.

THE GUSTATORY EXPERIENCE

The marinade flavors the food exposed to it:

✳ **by enriching the depth of flavor** of cooked or uncooked marinades.

✳ **by providing flavor** to the surface of the meat as it is served, in the case of instant marinades.

THE BEST TEA TO CHOOSE

Any tea can be used, but make sure that the aromatic power of the tea and the food are well matched. For example, a game dish easily stands up to an intensely smoky marinade, but the same tea would not be appropriate for use with fish.

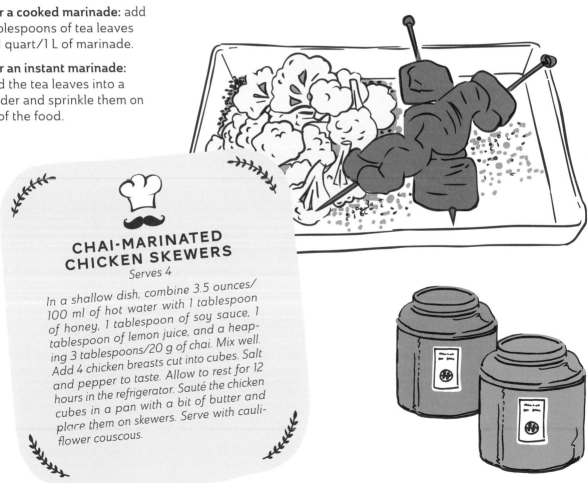

CHAI-MARINATED CHICKEN SKEWERS
Serves 4

In a shallow dish, combine 3.5 ounces/ 100 ml of hot water with 1 tablespoon of honey, 1 tablespoon of soy sauce, 1 tablespoon of lemon juice, and a heaping 3 tablespoons/20 g of chai. Mix well. Add 4 chicken breasts cut into cubes. Salt and pepper to taste. Allow to rest for 12 hours in the refrigerator. Sauté the chicken cubes in a pan with a bit of butter and place them on skewers. Serve with cauliflower couscous.

MAKING AN ASPIC

You can count on tea as a very dependable ingredient when making an aspic.
The immense variety of teas available offers a vast range of possibilities in terms of flavors and textures.

HOW TO
GO ABOUT IT

It's simple to make tea liquor into an aspic. **Use gelatin or agar-agar, depending on the effect you desire** and your preferences. Gelatin produces aspics that are soft and smooth, whereas agar-agar produces firmer, more "brittle" textures. For every 16 ounces/500 ml of tea, use 8 leaves/16 g of gelatin or ½ teaspoon/2 g of agar-agar.

THE GUSTATORY
EXPERIENCE

In an aspic, you'll capture the tastes and flavors that appear in the tea liquor itself. You can also adjust the taste by lightly adding salt, sugar, or any other seasoning to the tea that serves as the liquid base.

THE BEST TEA
TO CHOOSE

All types of tea, including flavored varieties, are suitable.

ASPIC OF
RED BERRIES WITH
JASMINE TEA
Serves 4

In a pot, infuse 13.5 ounces/400 ml of good-quality jasmine tea. Strain. Add sugar to taste and replace the pot over heat. Add 4 leaves/8 g of softened gelatin. When they have dissolved, let the aspic cool and, while still liquid, pour it over the fruit (about 21 ounces/600 g for 4 small bowls or molds). Refrigerate for about 2½ hours.

MAKING AN EMULSION

Tea can be readily infused in milk or cream. Fatty substances (oil, butter, egg yolks) efficiently capture the aromas of tea. Emulsions vastly expand the potential uses of tea: light sauces, whipped cream desserts, foams, etc.

HOW TO GO ABOUT IT

The traditional technique involves beating the preparation with a whisk. Now that siphons are making their appearance in kitchens, you can produce even airier textures that are incredibly light on the palate.

THE GUSTATORY EXPERIENCE

Using emulsions, you have the opportunity to explore all of the aromas of tea in textures ranging from the unctuousness of mayonnaise to the ethereal lightness of a foam.

THE BEST TEA TO CHOOSE

Any type of tea can be used.

PU ERH FOAM

In a pot, heat 13.5 ounces/400 ml of light whipping cream to 176°F/80°C. Infuse 3 tablespoons of Pu Erh in the cream for 3 minutes. Strain. Add salt and pepper to taste. Refrigerate. When the cream is chilled, add an egg yolk, then beat the mixture with a whisk. Correct the seasonings. Pour into a siphon, and use it to garnish a platter. You'll find that the foam is a delectable accompaniment to your dish. It's an airy complement with forest notes for poached eggs, foie gras, or a cold first course featuring mushrooms.

DUSTING WITH POWDERED TEA

Tea can be ground into a powder to serve as an ingredient.
Matcha, beloved by pastry chefs, is the most common example, but other teas can also be crushed and added to the recipe or sprinkled as a seasoning.

HOW TO GO ABOUT IT

There are many ways to grind tea, depending on what you intend to do with it:

* **use a mortar or a blender** if you're including the tea as a main ingredient in a preparation.

* **use a mill** with salt, pepper, or other spices if the tea is added to a condiment.

THE GUSTATORY EXPERIENCE

Tea can be used just like a spice. It enlivens a dish, adding character and a touch of originality to the recipe.

THE BEST TEA TO CHOOSE

Any tea can be ground into a powder and added to your cooking. Follow your impulses!

Chinese dark and black teas are ideal **for soups**.

For a vinaigrette, choose a Matcha or other green tea.

Consider flavored teas as **an addition to granulated sugar**.

FLEUR DE SEL WITH LAPSANG SOUCHONG

In a salt grinder, combine 1 part smoked tea to 9 parts fleur de sel. Ideal for seasoning salmon or scallop dishes.

SEL GRIS WITH MATCHA

Combine 2 tablespoons of coarse gray salt with 1/2 teaspoon of Matcha. You'll have a delicious salt with mild notes of bitterness and iodine that will extend your taste horizons.

REDUCING

An alternative to extracts (see page 191), reduction through evaporation concentrates tea's tastes. You can use this technique successfully with tea that's been infused in water, milk, or cream when deglazing a pan, for example.

HOW TO GO ABOUT IT

Warm the tea-based preparation, preferably in a covered pot. The reduction can then be used as the base for a sauce, or you can incorporate it as an ingredient in another recipe.

THE GUSTATORY EXPERIENCE

The aromas and tannins of the tea are concentrated, adding powerful flavor notes and texture to the reduction.

THE BEST TEA TO CHOOSE

Avoid very delicate teas such as green teas or lightly oxidized oolongs **when cooking down a reduction at high heat**.

Otherwise, any tea may be used.

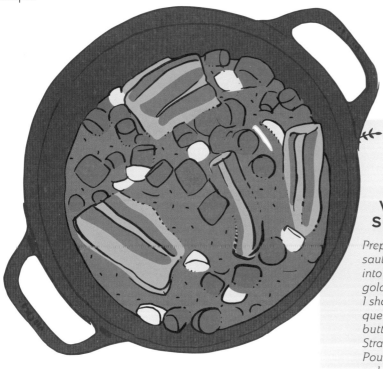

VEAL STEWED WITH SUMMER DARJEELING

Prepare 1½ quarts/1.5 L of tea. In a pan, sauté 2½ pounds/1.2 kg of veal flank cut into large cubes in a bit of oil until nicely golden brown. Add 1 onion, 1 carrot, and 1 shallot, all minced; 1 garlic clove; 1 bouquet garni; and 5 tablespoons/75 g of butter cut into pieces. Stir frequently. Strain. Set aside the veal and vegetables. Pour the strained liquid into a pan and reduce with about 3.5 ounces/100 ml of tea until it has a syrupy consistency. Add back the veal and vegetables. Simmer for 2 to 3 hours. Strain again and allow to reduce to the desired consistency. Do not add seasoning until you are ready to serve. A classic of French cuisine reimagined with tea!

DEGLAZING

The process of deglazing involves using a liquid to dissolve the browned bits remaining in a pan after cooking to make a jus or sauce. Tea makes a welcome change from wine, stock, bouillon, and vinegar.

HOW TO GO ABOUT IT

Remove the sautéed contents of the pan, and pour tea over the brown bits remaining on its surface. Using a spatula, loosen the brown bits and allow to dissolve for 3 to 4 minutes over low heat. Reduce the liquid to the concentration desired, and correct the seasonings.

THE GUSTATORY EXPERIENCE

Like any other deglazing liquid, tea brings its own personality to the browned, caramelized flavors of the sauté pan.

THE BEST TEA TO CHOOSE

If the contents of the pan are deeply browned, or even scorched, it's best to use a strong, highly concentrated variety, such as dark tea, Chinese or Assam black tea, or roasted teas. You could also try a bergamot-flavored black tea, which will add a zesty note to the dish.

If the pan's contents are just slightly browned (when cooking fish, for example), any green tea works well, and its delicate bouquet will survive the cooking process.

WOK-COOKED SQUID WITH SENCHA
Serves 4

In a small amount of oil, stir-fry 1 minced garlic clove, 2 minced onions, and 1¼ pounds/600 g of squid cut into strips for about 10 minutes, just until nicely browned. Add salt and pepper while cooking. Set the squid aside and keep warm. Pour 3.5 ounces/100 ml of Sencha green tea into the wok to deglaze it and reduce the liquid. Correct the seasoning of the reduction, and pour it over the squid. Scatter with a few leaves of parsley.

MAKING A SALT CRUST

Cooking food in a salt crust prevents it from drying out and makes it more tender.
Your dish will be even more savory if you include tea in the recipe.

HOW TO GO ABOUT IT

Incorporate dry tea leaves into the mixture of salt and egg whites for the crust. Nothing could be simpler.

THE GUSTATORY EXPERIENCE

The tea adds its flavor to the crust, which in turn conveys it to the food.

THE BEST TEA TO CHOOSE

Select the tea based on what you're preparing.

For white fish or poultry, choose green or lightly oxidized teas.

For game, use robust black or smoked teas.

SEA BASS IN A BAO ZHONG SALT CRUST

For a sea bass weighing 1¾ pounds/800 g

Preheat the oven to 400°F/200°C. Combine 6½ pounds/3 kg of coarse salt, 3 beaten egg whites, and 4 tablespoons of infused tea leaves. Cover a baking dish with parchment paper and spread with a layer of the egg white–salt–tea preparation (adding a little water if necessary). Arrange the fish (gutted, not scaled) on top and sprinkle with olive oil. Spread the fish with the remaining mixture so that it is completely covered. Bake for about 20 minutes and then allow to rest for 10 minutes before cracking open the crust. Use a jade green Matcha for a spectacular effect.

PIERCING AND SCORING

*To make sure the flavor penetrates all the way through
a piece of meat, fish, or vegetable, leaves of assertive teas can be
introduced directly into the food.*

HOW TO
GO ABOUT IT

Tea leaves are too fragile
to be pressed into a roast as
you might push cloves into
an onion. You'll have to score
or make holes in the meat,
fish, or vegetable so that you
can pack the tea leaves inside.
You can make small or large
cuts, depending on the
desired effect.

THE GUSTATORY
EXPERIENCE

The tea diffuses its aromas
inside the meat and adds a
subtle flavor.

THE BEST TEA
TO CHOOSE

Choose an assertive tea
for meats (a dark or Yunnan
black tea) that will add its
own personality to the rich
flesh and fat.

For fish and vegetables,
select teas with grassy, iodine
notes. Consider Chinese or
Japanese green teas or teas
with roasted flavors, such as
Hojicha.

DUCK BREAST WITH SMOKED TEA

*Using a knife, score the skin in a crisscross pattern. Press the tea
leaves into these incisions, and wrap the duck breast tightly in
plastic wrap. Refrigerate for at least 12 hours so that the fat
of the duck is thoroughly impregnated with the smoked tea
flavors.*

*Unwrap the duck breast and remove the tea leaves. Salt and
pepper both sides of the breast*

*In a very hot pan, without added fat, cook the breast, skin side
down, for 7 minutes, then turn over and cook for an additional
7 minutes. Serve when nicely crisp.*

BASTING

Is there leftover tea in your pot? Don't throw it out. Use it moisten a chicken, leg of lamb, or any other roast that benefits from a bit of basting while it cooks.

HOW TO GO ABOUT IT

Nothing could be simpler. Baste the roast with tea mixed with the cooking juices.

✳ For a chicken: add the tea to the pan at the beginning of the cooking time.

✳ For a beef roast: select an extract or very concentrated tea to mix with the cooking juices while the roast is in the oven.

✳ For a leg of lamb: combine equal parts tea with the lamb fat and juices. Baste every 15 minutes.

THE GUSTATORY EXPERIENCE

The flavors of the tea add a delicate aroma to the cooking juices, lending a novel touch to traditional recipes.

THE BEST TEA TO CHOOSE

Chose dark teas or Chinese or Assam black teas **for beef, lamb, or game**.

For chicken, try Chinese or Japanese green teas.

FOUR DELICIOUS BASTING LIQUIDS

With a roast chicken: a Long Jing

With a beef roast: a Yunnan Buds

With a leg of lamb: an Assam Maijian

With roast venison: a Pu Erh

MAKING AN EXTRACT OR CONCENTRATE

*What's the best way to add the flavor of your favorite tea to a recipe?
It's not always simple, because tea liquor doesn't work well in every sauce.
Sometimes, making an extract is by far the best solution.*

HOW TO GO ABOUT IT

Infuse a large amount of leaves in a very small amount of simmering water for 1 to 2 minutes. Allow a generous 3 tablespoons/20 g of tea for 3.5 ounces/100 ml of concentrate. Then add the liquor to your recipe.

THE GUSTATORY EXPERIENCE

In addition to adding the tea's own distinctive aromatic notes to enrich the dish, the extract's astringency will make the recipe's flavors linger in your mouth.

THE BEST TEA TO CHOOSE

If you are using the extract to boost the existing flavor of a dish, select a tea that is in the same flavor family as the recipe.

If the extract is intended to season the dish, choose a tea with the flavors you want to add.

GRAND OOLONG TOP FANCY CARAMEL

Prepare an extract by infusing 5 tablespoons/30 g of tea leaves in 5 ounces/150 ml of water at 203°F/95°C for 1 minute. Strain. Allow to cool. In a pot, combine the extract with 8¾ ounces/250 g of sugar and several drops of lemon juice. Cook down and caramelize as deeply as you wish. Perfect for flavoring a tarte Tatin!

SMOKING

Smoked tea is among your very best allies in the kitchen, since it's one of the very few ingredients that provides the popular flavor of smoky aromatic wood. It's the simple alternative when you don't want to deal with food flavorings or much more complicated smoking techniques.

HOW TO
GO ABOUT IT

Most of the techniques described earlier work well with smoked tea.

✷ Direct contact techniques: dry rubs, sprinkling…

✷ Immersion techniques: infusing, marinating…

✷ Incorporation techniques: extracts, deglazing…

THE GUSTATORY
EXPERIENCE

Smoked teas are very low in tannins, so they primarily convey notes of smokiness to the dish rather than the texture provided by the astringency of tannic teas.

THE BEST TEA
TO CHOOSE

Choose any Lapsang Souchong, from the mildest to the most assertive, depending on the effect you're after.

SMOKED SALMON
WITH LAPSANG SOUCHONG

Combine 3.5 ounces//100 g of coarse gray salt, 3 tablespoons/ 50 g of sugar, and 5 tablespoons/30 g of tea. Lay a fresh fillet of salmon (preferably Scottish or wild-caught Alaskan sockeye) on a sheet of plastic film, skin side down. Cover the flesh side with a layer of the salt-sugar-tea mixture about 1/16 inch/2 mm thick. Seal the plastic wrap tightly and refrigerate the fish for 1 day. Pour off the liquid released by the salmon frequently. Remove the salmon from its wrapping and rinse in cold water. Wipe carefully and return to the refrigerator uncovered. Serve the following day.

ADDING COLOR

*Tea liquors offer a color palette that can be attractive
for tinting or intensifying the hues of light-colored foodstuffs.
Tea can sometimes replace food colorings.*

HOW TO
GO ABOUT IT

It all depends on the food you want to color. There's no doubt that **white or transparent foods** lend themselves best, whether by being mixed with tea (milk, cream, flour, egg white, aspic) or absorbing it (rice).

Surface coloring works best with foods that can be soaked in tea for an extended period.

THE GUSTATORY
EXPERIENCE

Although the visual effect is your main concern, you should of course consider the impact on the taste.

THE BEST TEAS
TO CHOOSE

If you want a honey color, choose a summer Darjeeling or a Hojicha.

Select a dark tea **for a brown color**.

For an almost fluorescent green, use a Matcha (which mustn't be heated over 194°F/90°C to avoid having it turn an unappetizing shade of khaki green).

MATCHA WHIPPED
CREAM

Combine 3 tablespoons/50 g of sugar with 1 heaping teaspoon of Matcha. Whip 10 ounces/300 ml of very cold heavy cream until it firms, then add the sugar-tea mixture, beating continuously. The lovely celadon hue of the whipped cream is the perfect complement to red berry desserts.

MULTITASKING MATCHA

Matcha, the tea of the famed Japanese ceremony, is prized for its brilliant green hue, light powdery consistency, and delicate, grassy aroma. It makes a novel and delicious ingredient that is treasured in kitchens all over the world.

SPRINKLE IT ON A DISH

The simplest way to use Matcha is as a spice with infinite seasoning possibilities. Add to the flavor a vinaigrette, enliven a salt, powder a waffle, or season a fillet or shellfish. A sprinkle of Matcha just before serving can transform a dish.

INCLUDE IT IN A PASTRY RECIPE

Ground into a powder as fine as flour, Matcha can be easily incorporated into recipes using ground almonds, flour, confectioners' sugar, etc.

It is generally added in the proportion of between 5 and 20 percent of the weight of the powder ingredient.

When heated, Matcha's luminous green hue assumes more or less vivid shades, depending on the cooking temperature.

USE IT TO FLAVOR AND COLOR A CUSTARD OR SORBET

So long as the cooking temperature does not exceed 176° to 194°F/80° to 90°C, Matcha retains all of its distinctive flavor and color traits. Combined with whipping cream, milk, simple syrup, or any other liquid, it is a 100 percent natural food coloring that contributes a distinctive fresh aroma with iodine notes. Its faint bitterness is one of its appealing qualities. Used judiciously, it makes a lovely Matcha ice cream.

MATCHA MERINGUES

Preheat the oven to 200°F/100°C. In a large bowl, combine 1 tablespoon/6 g of Matcha with 7 ounces/200 g of sugar. Using a beater or whisk, beat 3.5 ounces/100 g of egg whites until they form soft peaks. As they begin to thicken, add the Matcha-flavored sugar in three parts, continuing to beat. When the egg whites form almost stiff peaks, they are ready. Using a pastry bag, form the meringues into the desired shape. Bake for 45 minutes.

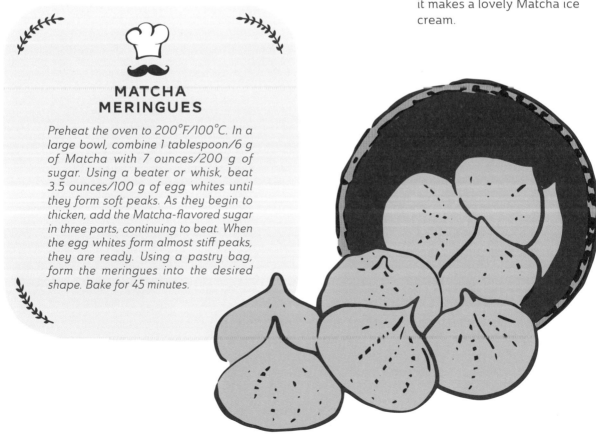

TEA-BASED COCKTAILS

*Tea is rarely mixed with other beverages, except punch or iced tea,
but it can nevertheless hold its own in sophisticated cocktails. Tea, particularly flavored varieties,
expands the range of interesting nonalcoholic ingredients.*

CHAMPAGNE WITH THÉ DU HAMMAM
Makes 5 flutes

Infuse 1 tablespoon/6 g of the tea in 10 ounces/300 ml of 176°F/80°C water for 3 minutes. Strain. Chill in the refrigerator. Pour the tea together with 1½ tablespoons/25 ml of peach liqueur into a shaker and shake vigorously. Fill the flutes halfway and top up with iced Champagne

HOW TO GO ABOUT IT

There are three main techniques:

✳ **Tea liquor:** infuse tea following the instructions on page 22 and let it cool before adding to a cocktail.

✳ **Extract:** follow the instructions on page 191, and allow it to cool.

✳ **Macerate tea directly in alcohol:** it can serve as a cocktail base because it has a long shelf life (at least 5 days if infused in vodka, for example).

THE GUSTATORY EXPERIENCE

The key to a good cocktail is the right balance among the various ingredients. You have to take great care in getting the correct proportion for each component. The right amount of tea extract or liquor will contribute flavor as well as astringency, along with a pleasant hint of bitterness.

THE BEST TEA TO CHOOSE

Use any tea that develops a certain degree of aromatic intensity. Flavored teas are particularly useful because they contribute aromatic notes that are difficult to obtain with juices or alcohol.

BECOMING
A TEA
SOMMELIER

WHAT MAKES AN ACCOMPLISHED TEA SOMMELIER?

You don't have to be gifted with elite powers of taste and smell to earn distinction in the realm of tea tasting. These senses are usually so understimulated that, even with limited training, you can make rapid progress. However, certain qualities are invaluable for anyone seeking to become a tea sommelier.

A PASSION FOR TEA AND INSATIABLE CURIOSITY

If you decide to become a tea sommelier, tea almost certainly already plays an important role in your life. This passion is certainly your most important resource, because it stimulates your desire to learn. The world of tea is so wide that it takes tremendous curiosity to explore it thoroughly.

AN EXCELLENT MEMORY

Indisputably, there are more varieties of tea in the world than wine. That fact gives you a notion of the scope of knowledge required of a tea sommelier!

Finding your way among the major categories of tea, analyzing the taste of a tea to categorize it by family, knowing how to discuss a grand cru as easily as a daily brew—all these tasks require a formidable base of knowledge. Your expertise must be multifaceted: you have to be able to identify tastes and aromas as well as call upon extensive theoretical knowledge, while mastering the specialized terminology related to tea tasting.

A LOVE OF TEACHING AND A DESIRE TO SHARE YOUR KNOWLEDGE

The tea sommelier is not a recluse who samples infusions in isolation. The profession's mission is to provide advice and convey skills and expertise. Good sommeliers know how to share their passion and knowledge, making the information accessible to others and speaking on their level.

THE ROLE OF THE TEA SOMMELIER

Tea sommeliers are the tea specialists in gourmet restaurants and luxury hotels. They may also act as experts and provide advice in tea boutiques or specialty grocery shops. They often play multiple roles:

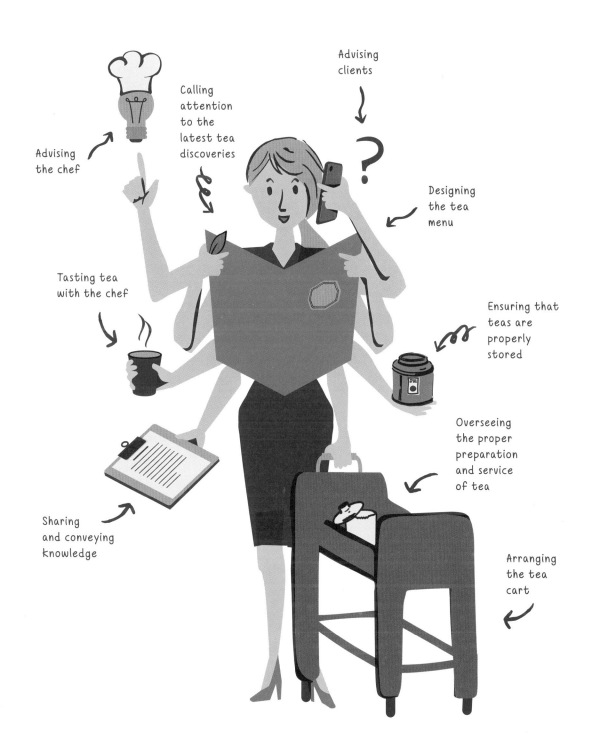

Advising the chef

Calling attention to the latest tea discoveries

Advising clients

Tasting tea with the chef

Designing the tea menu

Ensuring that teas are properly stored

Sharing and conveying knowledge

Overseeing the proper preparation and service of tea

Arranging the tea cart

PROFESSIONAL OPPORTUNITIES FOR A TEA SOMMELIER

The métier of tea sommelier—a recognized profession in some countries, such as China, Russia, and Korea—is beginning to develop in the West and is gradually assuming a more prominent place in the world of gastronomy. Although full-time tea sommelier positions are still rare, the expertise is in increasingly great demand.

IN A HIGH-END RESTAURANT

It's often forgotten that wine sommeliers are also responsible for tea and are increasingly expected to be knowledgeable on the subject. They have to have informed advice on the tip of their tongue and respond to the expectations of both chefs and patrons. If you are equally passionate about tea and wine, make sure you employ your double expertise in the earliest stages of your professional training.

IN A LUXURY HOTEL

In these establishments, tea is available in multiple locations all day long: breakfast, brunch, high tea, in the salon, bar, bedrooms, and in reception areas and meeting places. The sommelier has a broad role in overseeing wines if the hotel has a restaurant, and is also the person responsible for selecting and purchasing tea as well as other beverages.

IN A TEAHOUSE

In most countries, the tea business is booming, and specialized teahouses offer top-quality products for sale (grands crus, house specialties, etc.). These boutiques are proliferating and have established themselves in growing numbers of cultural capitals and cities. These establishments are veritable palaces dedicated to the celebration of tea, and tea sommeliers are essential for advising clients and training knowledgeable teams of employees.

NOW HIRING
TEA SOMMELIER

TRUE OR FALSE?

Have you mastered the basics for becoming a tea sommelier?
Have fun testing yourself. You'll find complete answers to all these questions
in the chapters of this book.

Green and black teas
come from two different
plants.

☐ true ☐ false

*False. Green and black teas
are determined by the process used to
treat the leaves after the harvest
(see page 73).*

Some teas are
suited to being infused
several times.

☐ true ☐ false

*True. This is the case for teas
prepared following the
Gong Fu Cha method (see page 62).*

A tea infused in
cold water will be much
lower in caffeine.

☐ true ☐ false

*True. The hotter the water,
the more caffeine dissolves
(see page 56).*

Black teas are
fermented teas.

☐ true ☐ false

*False. Black teas are oxidized
(see pages 74–75). Dark teas, also
known as Pu Erhs in China, are the
only ones actually fermented
(see page 82–83).*

There are five tastes:
sweet, salty, sour, bitter,
and umami.

☐ true ☐ false

True. (see page 43).

To infuse a tea
at room temperature,
it should be steeped
for 24 hours.

☐ true ☐ false

*False. One hour is sufficient
(see page 26).*

Some teas have
iodine flavors.

☐ true ☐ false

*True. Japanese green teas are
known for aromas that evoke the
ocean (see pages 153 and 162).*

If tea is left to infuse
for too long, it may become
too sweet.

☐ true ☐ false

*False. If allowed to steep too long,
some teas become bitter
(see page 21).*

A Chinese green tea
is the perfect
accompaniment to
a fresh goat cheese.

☐ true ☐ false

*True. A Chinese green tea
or lightly oxidized oolong pairs
beautifully with goat cheeses
(see page 166).*

Dark teas (Pu Erhs)
go well with delicate
fish recipes.

☐ true ☐ false

*False. Pu Erhs have very
powerful aromas (see page 162).
A Japanese green tea would
be a better choice.*

LIFELONG LEARNING

You'll find that you make very rapid progress as you begin to learn the techniques of tea tasting. You may be surprised that no particular innate ability is required to stimulate your underused senses. But if you wish to become a tea sommelier, you'll have to make a genuine commitment to the profession, tirelessly seeking out and tasting the world's great teas.

THE CHALLENGES

Our senses come alive when we taste a tea (see page 38). They gather numerous bits of information and transmit them to the brain, which interprets this input and connects the data, ultimately deriving a distinctive impression of the tea being tasted. Finally, the brain reinterprets this image in the form of emotions and words.

This is where training counts, because deconstructing and detailing this unique image is no simple task. It's not easy to separate one sensation from another, or determine the appropriate order for tasting or tactile experiences (it's easy to confuse bitterness and astringency, for example). Untangling the web of sensations requires intense concentration and linguistic precision. The process of verbalization teaches us to recognize nuances and give detailed expression to our impressions.

OVERCOMING THE INITIAL EMOTIONAL REACTION

When we are confronted with a taste or smell, we have a spontaneous reaction: "I like/don't like it"; "It's good/not good"; "That smells good/bad"; "This reminds me of..." Getting past this immediate emotional reaction requires conscious effort and discipline. Although the most intriguing aspect of a tasting may be the emotions that are stirred, it's essential to know how to distance yourself, so as to focus on the sensations and describe each of them with the utmost precision.

FINE-TUNING YOUR SENSES

Giving methodical expression to sensations by naming them—deploying the most precise terminology available—allows the student to progress in the art of tasting. The more specific and nuanced the description of impressions, the more richness and pleasure you'll experience. While you gain experience in providing precise descriptions, your sensations will become more refined and perceptive as you cultivate your senses of taste and smell.

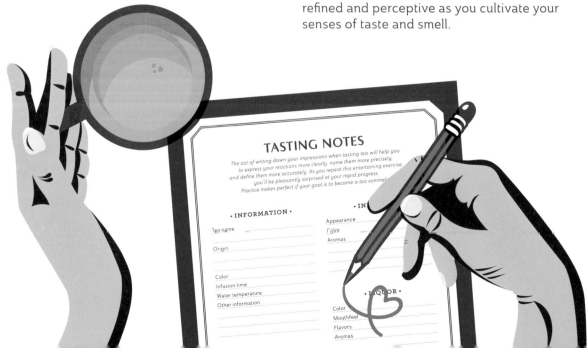

TASTING NOTES

The act of writing down your impressions when tasting tea will help you to express your reactions more clearly, name them more precisely, and define them more accurately. As you repeat this entertaining exercise, you'll be pleasantly surprised at your rapid progress. Practice makes perfect if your goal is to become a tea sommelier.

• INFORMATION •

Tea name

Origin

Color
Infusion time
Water temperature
Other information

• INFORMATION •

Appearance
Color
Aromas

• LIQUOR •

Color
Mouthfeel
Flavors
Aromas

SPIT OR SWALLOW?

In some tastings, you'll sample just a few teas and swallow the liquor.
But if you have several dozen cups in front of you, you'll obviously have to spit.

WHY SWALLOW?

✳ For the most complete tasting experience possible.

✳ For pleasure!

WHY SPIT?

If you're tasting many different teas, there are numerous advantages to spitting:

✳ **You drink a much smaller quantity of liquid.**

✳ **You are less sensitive to bitterness** because you position yourself with your head bent forward, ready to spit. Taste buds for bitterness are concentrated at the back of your mouth (see page 43).

✳ **You are less sensitive to the tea's astringency** because the liquid is kept in your mouth for a shorter period of time.

✳ **You'll taste faster.** Not only will you move more rapidly from one tea to the next, but you'll also be able to taste a greater number without variations of temperature.

✳ **You'll be less influenced by the teas tasted before** because they will have had less opportunity to affect your mouth and throat.

ORGANIZING TASTINGS

The most pleasant and efficient way to perfect your tasting skills is to work in small groups. Conversing and sharing impressions will help enhance your experience and build your knowledge.

PROTOCOL FOR GROUP TASTINGS

For the best results, it's advisable to follow a few rules when organizing a tea tasting:

✳ Choose a theme for the tasting

If each participant brings a favorite tea to share with the others, set a theme (for example: black teas, Chinese teas, etc.). That will make it easier to focus attention on learning and apprenticeship, and not just sharing impressions.

Ideally, the job of selecting the teas to be tasted is assigned to one individual.

✳ Taste several teas

It's best to taste a least two teas to benefit from making comparisons. Keep in mind that making such comparisons often leads you to focus on differences, while neglecting to note common traits.

✳ Use the right equipment

The versatile tasting set (see page 42) is ideal. Use as many sets as you have teas to taste. You can also use small (10-ounce/300 ml) teapots and cups. In this case, choose small cups—containing one or two swallows—and avoid mugs. If your tasting is focused on a mode of preparation (Gong Fu Cha or Kyusu, for example), use traditional utensils.

✳ Slurp

The term for this approach to tasting speaks for itself—it calls for a noisy gulp. Slurping multiplies the sensations of retronasal olfaction. Get comfortable with each other at the beginning of the session. Abandon your inhibitions by starting the tasting with a resounding collective ritual slurp!

COMMUNICATE TO MAKE PROGRESS

Learning to communicate your impressions with others will give you an incentive to name them with greater precision and go into further detail than if you were tasting alone. When it comes to olfactory and gustatory sensations, our vocabulary is surprisingly imprecise. Sharing thoughts forces us to focus and refine our descriptions.

THREE ESSENTIAL RULES

✳ Except for the slurp, perform the tasting in silence to avoid influencing your neighbors (see page 53).

✳ Note your impressions on a tasting sheet (see page 59).

✳ And, of course, skip the perfume on a tasting day (see page 207).

PROGRESSIVE TASTINGS

Here are a few examples of possible themes, based on the group's level of expertise.

✳ **For beginners**
- The colors of tea: 1 white tea, 1 green tea, 1 black tea, 1 oolong, and 1 dark tea
- Classic teas: 1 green tea, 1 black tea, 1 breakfast tea, 1 flavored Earl Grey tea, 1 smoked tea, and 1 jasmine tea
- The countries of tea: 1 tea from China, 1 tea from Japan, 1 tea from India, 1 tea from Nepal, and 1 tea from Sri Lanka

✳ **For connoisseurs**
- 5 Japanese teas: 1 Sencha, 1 Gyokuro, 1 Tamaryokucha, 1 Hojicha, and 1 Genmaicha
- 5 black teas: 1 spring Darjeeling, 1 Yunnan, 1 Qimen, 1 Assam, and 1 black Nepal
- 5 oolongs: 1 classic Tie Guan Yin, 1 Bao Zhong, 1 Oriental Beauty, 1 Da Hong Pao, and 1 Geng Huang Dan Cong
- 5 green teas: 1 Sencha, 1 Long Jing, 1 Nepal green tea, 1 raw Pu Erh, and 1 African green tea

✳ **For experts**
- 5 spring Darjeelings
- 5 Himalayan black teas (spring, summer, and autumn harvests)
- 3 Lightly oxidized Taiwanese oolongs
- 3 Sencha Ichibancha teas

BLIND TASTINGS

To spice up your tasting experience, replace the tasting sets with black wineglasses.

You're sure to be challenged and perplexed!

THE TEA SOMMELIER'S KIT

Whether novice or professional, every tea sommelier requires a few essential utensils.
This collection can be enhanced with the addition of more specialized items as necessary.

ESSENTIALS

tasting sets

a thermometer
(for checking
the tasting
temperature)

a scale
accurate to
0.1 g

a timer

good water
(spring or
filtered)

a kettle with
an adjustable
thermostat

SPECIALIZED ACCESSORIES

a Kyusu

a Zhong

a Matcha bowl and whisk

a Gong Fu Cha teapot, pot,
and small cups

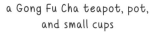

THE TEA SOMMELIER'S SWORN ENEMIES

As a professional taster in the service of fine tea, the tea sommelier must shun olfactory pollutants that could spoil the tasting experience. Offensive smells can come from the environment, the water used for preparing the tea, or the tea utensils and accessories.

BEST AVOIDED

Perfumes
It's the golden rule for any self-respecting tea sommelier: no perfume on the job. Avoid anything that might distract the senses of the sommelier or the clients.

Toothpaste
Toothpastes are often flavored with menthol or anise, and these components affect the taste buds for several hours after use. Avoid toothpaste within two hours of a tasting.

Odors on the hands (cigarettes, moisturizers, etc.)
Contrary to received wisdom, smoking is not an absolute taboo. There are smokers among the most accomplished tea tasters. Still, if you smoke, tobacco is the first odor you'll experience when you raise the cup to your lips. The odor may also contaminate the cup, which could be quite unpleasant in a group tasting.

A stuffy nose
This ailment obliterates retronasal olfaction. Just take care of yourself and do something else until you recover!

Chlorine and calcium
These are the Public Enemies Number I of tea and are therefore despised by tea sommeliers.

Ambient odors, particularly coffee
Avoid serving a grand cru tea near freshly roasted coffee.

Cleaning products
One of the great disadvantages of detergents is their persistent smell. To avoid this pitfall, take proper care of your equipment (see page 30).

DESIGNING A TEA MENU

Among the tea sommelier's duties is drawing up a list of teas to be included in the establishment's tea menu.

HOW TO DESIGN A TEA MENU

There are two steps to designing a tea menu:

* **First, decide on the number of selections to offer:** this decision will be based on the space allocated to tea within the beverage menu, as well as the restaurant's business model and the makeup of the clientele.

* **Choose the teas:** there are two possible approaches.

If you wish to satisfy the expectations of the maximum number of clients, your selection will include an equal number of plain and flavored teas.

The essentials: 1 smoked, 1 bergamot-scented tea, 1 green tea, 1 evening tea, 1 tea for those who like to add milk, 1 mint tea, 1 tea that aids digestion, and all the standards (Darjeeling, Sri Lanka, etc.).

If you are able to discuss your fascination with tea and explain your choices to the clientele, your tea selection can be more focused, like that of a wine connoisseur.

The essentials: this selection, which offers more scope for exploration, will include the grands crus of the moment and seasonal specialties that reflect the most recently harvested tea crops.

HELPFUL HINT

Allow a little extra time before you finalize your tea menu to take account of your clients' tastes. When you've been open for several weeks, you'll be in a position to consider the preferences and passions of your regular patrons.

TEA MENU

PROFESSIONAL TEA SERVICE

*The tea sommelier must give careful consideration
to the way tea is presented to guests. Tea service involves several steps,
each of which has very specific logistical implications.*

SELECTING A TEA

Several considerations may help the guest make a selection, in addition to assistance provided by the tea sommelier:

✽ **a tea menu:** This is very helpful to guests, allowing them to have an overview of the selections available and perhaps decide on what they'd like to order.

✽ **a selection of leaves to smell:** Offered in small containers set out on a cart or tray, their fragrance stimulates curiosity and an interest in tasting. This presentation is often reserved for formal dining situations, because it requires additional time and space.

THERMOS AND COFFEE ALERT!
✖

In certain situations—meetings and receptions, for example— the tea sommelier may need to use a thermos, either for keeping a supply of hot water handy or for maintaining the tea at the proper temperature. A thermos that is used for tea or water must never have been used for coffee. Even if it has been well washed, the lingering odors would never be acceptable to a tea connoisseur.

PREPARATION

Except when the tasting is a ceremonial event carried out in the guest's presence (using the Gong Fu Cha method or a Kyusu teapot), preparation usually begins in the kitchen. The tea is measured, the water is heated, and the infusion process begins. The tea sommelier then has two options:

✽ **the tea is presented to the client while the infusion is in progress:** There must be a way to stop the process at the right moment (using a timer, for example, with a little saucer where the strainer and the leaves can be placed when the infusion is complete).

✽ **or the tea is presented when the infusion is complete:** In addition to the teapot, the sommelier might bring an attractive container holding the infused leaves. This extra touch offers the patron the option of sniffing the leaves while assuring the most skeptical client that they have been used only once. When you serve the tea fully prepared, always pour the first cup for each guest.

BASIC QUESTIONS

*A tea sommelier must master all of the information included in this book
and be able to respond to any questions that might be asked by
a client, the chef, or the senior bartender.*

What tea would you recommend for drinking in the morning?

I'd like a light tea. What would you advise? (This question requires you to determine whether the client is looking for a tea that is low in caffeine, that is only mildly astringent, or that has very mild aromas—three very different questions.)

I'd like to try tea without adding milk/sugar. Which tea would be a good choice?

What tea goes with this dish?

**FREQUENTLY
ASKED
QUESTIONS**

I'm trying to cut back on coffee drinking. What would you advise us an alternative?

I'm worried that tea will keep me awake. Do you have a tea that would suit?

I'm looking for a tea that will help my digestion. What do you suggest?

I'd like a very flavorful tea. What would you suggest? (This question requires you to determine whether the client is looking for a naturally aromatic single source tea or a tea flavored with the addition of essential oils, for example.)

Is there a tea that my husband (who drinks his tea with a splash of milk) and I would both enjoy?

THE TEA SOMMELIER'S REFERENCE LIBRARY

Here's a list of works that will be valuable for any tea sommelier, whether expert or novice. Refer to these books to deepen your knowledge and enhance your enjoyment of the world of tea.

✳ To deepen your knowledge of the world of tea (the plant, its cultivation, its fabrication) and the science of tasting, consult the reference work by François-Xavier Delmas, Mathias Minet, and Christian Barbaste, *The Tea Drinker's Handbook* (New York: Abbeville Press, 2008). It is the fruit of our thirty years' experience in studying our favorite beverage.

✳ To follow in the footsteps of a tea adventurer, see Robert Fortune's *A Journey to the Tea Countries of China, Including Sung-Lo and the Bohea Hills* (London: Forgotten Books, 2015).

✳ For a botanical and agricultural reference, refer to Denis Bonheure's little book *Tea* (London: Macmillan Education, 1991).

✳ To explore Japan's intimate ties with tea, you'll find Kakuzô Okakura, *The Book of Tea* (London: Penguin, 2016); or Sen Sôshitsu, *The Japanese Way of Tea* (New York: Weatherhill, 1994) of great interest.

✳ For a helpful overview of the traditions of tea in China, see John Blofeld, *The Chinese Art of Tea* (Boston: Shambhala, 1997).

✳ Finally, in the interests of comprehensiveness and tradition, seek out the classic volume first published in 1935 by William H. Ukers, *All About Tea* (Mansfield Center, CT: Martino, 2007). It was for many years the definitive encyclopedic work on tea. It's no longer in print, so you'll have to haunt used bookshops or websites selling secondhand books to track it down.

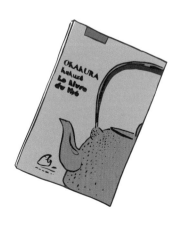

TRAINING AT THE ÉCOLE DU THÉ

Currently, tea sommelier qualifications are not taught within the official French educational system. However, the École du Thé of the Palais des Thés has been providing training in Paris since 1999, offering curricula focusing on the science of tea tasting. In 2016, the École du Thé began to offer a degree in tea sommelier studies, originally designed for professionals and soon to be available to the public.

TRAINING THAT'S ACCESSIBLE TO ALL

We're convinced that everyone is capable of appreciating the subtlety of a Chinese green tea and comparing two Himalayan grands crus harvested a few days apart. For seventeen years, we've been sharing expertise by offering beginner tea-tasting classes. This was the origin of the École du Thé.

Over the years, we have developed a curriculum that emphasizes sensory experience, based on an innovative pedagogical approach. Our classes emphasize the relationship between olfaction and taste, and they foster the progressive development of increasing tasting expertise.

A COMPLETE DEGREE PROGRAM

Students engage in detailed exploration of tea in the course of these studies, gradually mastering tasting techniques and learning the terminology. They acquire the entire compendium of knowledge of the tea sommelier. Teaching at the École du Thé is based upon five levels and a specifically designed curriculum:

LEVEL 1
Introductory steps into the world of tea
✖

This is the first essential exposure before starting an apprenticeship in tea. Traveling across the world through a sequence of images, the student is led through the universe of plantations all over the world, exploring tea, its history, and its civilization.

LEVEL 2
An apprenticeship in tea and tasting
✖

This series of twelve classes constitutes the basis of the apprenticeship program of the École du Thé. It provides an introduction to all aspects of tea and its tasting: knowledge of the tea plant and its transformation, techniques of preparation, familiarization with the mechanisms of tasting, and exploration of the most important tea producing nations.

LEVEL 3
Practical sessions on olfaction and taste
✖

Once a student has mastered the basics of tasting, practical training can begin. These sessions are built around a pedagogical approach that is proprietary to the École du Thé. It emphasizes the close connection between olfaction and tasting. Classes are organized around tastings of a series of teas. The objective is to learn to distinguish the various nuances of each. Samples of the teas tasted are handed out to students at the end of the class so that they can pursue their studies at home.

LEVEL 4
A deeper dive into tea tasting
⋈

For the most seasoned tasters, the École du Thé offers blind tastings involving the exploration of a series of four or five teas without any additional information than what is revealed by tasting. Organized by François-Xavier Delmas, these seminars give participants the opportunity to receive his advice and benefit from his knowledge.

LEVEL 5
Lose yourself in the world of tea
⋈

Taught by outside professionals—historians, chefs, recognized authorities on tea—and addressing topics related to the art and civilization of tea, these conferences give students the opportunity to meet others who are equally fascinated by tea and are recognized for their expertise.

THE TEA SOMMELIER DEGREE COURSE

Encompassing courses on all five levels, it is specifically designed for students who have decided to become professional tea sommeliers.

PASSING AN EXAMINATION AND EARNING A TEA SOMMELIER DEGREE

Since 2016, the École du Thé has awarded its degree of Tea Sommelier to qualified candidates. These graduates have completed the specific course of study and passed theoretical and practical examinations to demonstrate their mastery of the subject.

To find out more: www.ecoleduthe.com (in French)

THE TEA SOMMELIER'S GLOSSARY

Aroma: in the technical terminology of tea tasting, this word is reserved for the olfactory sensations perceived in the mouth during the process of retronasal olfaction. However, it is also frequently used to refer to smells in general.

Aromatic palette: the full range of the notes perceived in the liquor.

Aromatic profile: the ensemble of aromatic characteristics of a tea, considered from a dynamic rather than static perspective. It embraces the fleetingness of the notes (top notes, heart notes, and base notes) and often the effect of the texture and the flavors on the balance of the liquor.

Aromatic: refers to a strong liquor with powerful flavors.

Astringency: a harsh or rough quality in the mouth. Sometimes a sensation of dryness due to tannins.

Attack: refers to the notes initially perceived through direct or retronasal olfaction.

Balanced: describes a liquor whose aromas follow one another smoothly, complemented by the tea's flavors and texture.

Body: aspect of a liquor that combines a strong structure (robust liquor) and a sense of density. Adj.: full-bodied.

Bouquet: the ensemble of smells perceived by the nose.

Complex: describes a rich bouquet in terms of the number and subtlety of the aromas.

Creamy: refers to a tea that is round in the mouth and slightly oily.

Dense: refers to a liquor whose viscosity seems greater than that of water, suggesting an oily or creamy quality.

Dominant: refers to the family of aromas that are predominant in the liquor.

Finish: refers to the final notes perceived by direct or retronasal olfaction.

Frank: describes a tea whose characteristics (texture, flavors, aromas, etc.) are well defined and expressed cleanly, without ambiguity.

Full in the mouth: giving a sensation of fullness that has a pleasing mouth-filling effect. Also see "Roundness."

Full: describes a full, rounded liquor whose aromas pervade the mouth.

Grand cru: "great production," or tea of the finest quality.

Harmony: describes an appealing balance of taste, texture, and aromas, with a pleasing sequence of notes.

Infusion: describes both the act of infusing and the wet leaves recovered from the process. In the case of tea, the infusion is not the liquid obtained from the infusion process. (This is called the liquor.)

Intense: expressed powerfully and lastingly.

Liquor: liquid obtained by infusing tea leaves.

Long in the mouth: used for a tea whose aromas leave an agreeable and long-lasting impression in the front and back of the mouth after tasting.

Mild: said of a liquor with no astringency, whose flavor is mildly sweet. A characteristic sometimes associated with vanilla aromas.

Monolithic: describes a narrow aromatic palette, experienced as a single impression.

Mouth: the ensemble of sensations perceived in the mouth.

Nose: see Bouquet.

Note: synonymous with aroma.

Oily: describes a liquor whose texture is reminiscent of oil, with various degrees of finesse.

Opulent: describes a rich, heavy tea, often a heady brew.

Peak: describes the notes of a tea perceived in fits and starts.

Persistence: describes aromas that linger in the mouth.

Powdery: describes a liquor whose delicate astringency leaves a sensation of fine powder in the mouth.

Robust: refers to a liquor with prominent tannins that fills the mouth well.

Rough: describes a very astringent tea, often of inferior quality or else infused far too long.

Roundness: describes a liquor whose flavors fill the mouth fully.

Short in the mouth: a tea that leaves few traces of flavor in the front and back of the mouth after tasting.

Silky: describes a supple, slightly oily liquor, evocative of silk.

Smooth: describes a liquor with no harshness due to the absence of "heavy" tannins.

Sturdy: describes a tea whose structure is very robust. This quality can be moderated by adding milk.

Supple: said of a liquor whose mellowness dominates its astringency.

Tannic: refers to a liquor rich in tannins (also called "polyphenols").

Velvety: said of a slightly dense liquor that suggests the texture of velvet.

Vivacious: refers to a fresh, light liquor with a slight sourness that is not overwhelming, very pleasing to the palate.

INDEX

The page numbers in roman type refer to simple mentions of the term listed; those in bold to more explanatory entries; and those in italic to place names or tea symbols appearing on maps. Tea names followed by an asterisk (*) indicate registered trademarks of the Palais des Thés.

DETAILED CONTENTS

LIST OF RECIPES

CREDITS

ACKNOWLEDGMENTS

THE AUTHORS WOULD LIKE TO THANK
Bénédicte Bortoli for her invaluable assistance,
her always insightful comments, her commitment,
and her extraordinary expertise and responsiveness.
We also thank Bénédicte Carlou
for her efficient daily oversight of thousands—even tens of thousands—
of tea tastings each year,
and her unfailingly diplomatic and proficient support.
Thanks also to Lauriane Tiberghien
for animating our words
with her delightful drawings.

THE ILLUSTRATOR THANKS
Sabine and Valérie for their serene confidence in the face of every challenge;
Nicolas, Élodie, and Bénédicte for their deeply valued assistance;
and François-Xavier and Mathias who so delectably
convey their love of tea to others.

For the original edition
GENERAL MANAGER: Fabienne Kriegel
EDITORIAL DIRECTOR: Valérie Tognali
EDITOR: Bénédicte Bortoli
ART DIRECTION:
Sabine Houplain, assisted by Élodie Palumbo
GRAPHIC DESIGN AND ILLUSTRATIONS:
Lauriane Tiberghien
PRODUCTION: Marion Lance

For the English-language edition
PROJECT EDITOR: Mary Christian
COPY EDITOR: Iris Bass
PROOFREADER: Peggy Paul Casella
COMPOSITION: Angela Taormina
PRODUCTION MANAGER:
Louise Kurtz

First published in the United States of America in 2018 by
Abbeville Press, 655 Third Avenue, New York, NY 10017

First published in France in 2016 by Éditions du Chêne, 58 rue Jean Bleuzen, 92170 Vanves

First edition
3 5 7 9 10 8 6 4

Library of Congress Cataloging-in-Publication Data
Names: Delmas, Francois-Xavier, author. | Minet, Mathias, author.
Title: Tea sommelier : a step-by-step guide / Francois-Xavier Delmas,
Mathias Minet.
Other titles: Guide de degustation de l'amateur de the. English
Description: First edition. | New York : Abbeville Press,, 2018. | Originally
published in French under title: Guide de degustation de l'amateur de
the. Vanves : Editions du Chene, 2016. | Includes bibliographical
references and index.
Identifiers: LCCN 2018023569 | ISBN 9780789213129 (hardcover : alk. paper)
Subjects: LCSH: Tea—Guidebooks. | Tea—History. | Tea tasting.
Classification: LCC TX817.T3 D513 2018 | DDC 641.87/7—dc23
LC record available at https://lccn.loc.gov/2018023569

For bulk and premium sales and for text adoption procedures, write to Customer Service Manager,
Abbeville Press, 655 Third Avenue, New York, NY 10017, or call 1-800-ARTBOOK.

Visit Abbeville Press online at www.abbeville.com.